W9-CZB-689

ACTIONS SPEAK!

How to Conduct
a Behavior-Based Interview

Paul C. Green, Ph.D.

MEDIA LEARNING INTERNATIONAL LLC

ACTIONS SPEAK!
How to Conduct a Behavior-Based Interview

Media Learning International LLC
1173 Glen Oaks Drive
Des Moines, IA 50266

Copyright © 2012 by Media Learning International LLC. All rights reserved.

Printed in the United States of America.

Portions of this book were adapted from *Get Talent: Interview for Actions, Select for Results.* Copyright © 2007 by Paul C. Green, Ph.D. Inc. (AKA Skilfast Inc.) ALL RIGHTS RESERVED.

Permission to reproduce or transmit in any form or by any means, electronic or mechanical, including photocopying and recording, or by an information storage and retrieval system, must be obtained in writing from the author by contacting the publisher.

The information contained in this book and related materials is subject to change without notice. Media Learning International LLC, Paul C. Green, Ph.D. Inc., and Paul C. Green make no warranty of any kind with regard to this material, including, but not limited to, the implied warranties of merchantability and fitness for a particular purpose, including training or workforce selection. Media Learning International LLC, Paul C. Green, Ph.D. Inc., and Paul C. Green shall not be liable for omissions or errors contained herein or for incidental or consequential damages in connection with the furnishing, performance, or use of this material in any manner whatsoever.

Ordering Information

To order additional copies, contact Paul Green at **paulcgreen.com**. Quantity discounts are available.

For more information, visit **medialearninginternational.com**.

ISBN (paperback) 978-0-9848116-0-1

Credits

Managing editor: Jeff Morris
Proofreader: Deborah Costenbader
Text design: Jeff Morris
Cover design: Art Bauer

First printing: January 2012

For . . .

my Mom,

who spoke of how things could be, and . . .

my Dad,

who taught how words shape what will be.

CONTENTS

ABOUT THE AUTHOR

Paul Green is an industrial-organizational psychologist with over 40 years of experience in training and consulting. He built one of the largest professional practices in the United States, with an emphasis on the assessment of job candidates. Over a 20-year period he conducted more than 5,000 interviews for candidates in a broad range of jobs. Based on this experience, he developed the Behavioral Interviewing Seminar in the early 1980s and subsequently led one of the largest interview training companies in the world.

His writing has been published in several formats, including *Get Hired: Winning Strategies to Ace the Interview* (Bard Press), *Building Robust Competencies: Linking Human Resource Systems to Organizational Strategies* (Jossey-Bass), *Get Talent: Interview for Actions, Select for Results* (SkilFast), and *101 Interviews for the Most Common Jobs in America* (in press: Media Learning International LLC). In addition, Paul has been the technical expert, on-screen talent, or co-producer of nine training videos on interviewing and problem solving, including an all-time bestseller, as described in *FORTUNE* magazine.

Currently, Paul is a co-owner of Media Learning International LLC, a Des Moines–based e-learning/video production company whose mission is to find good ideas and communicate them. Paul continues to speak at corporate events, coach interviewers and candidates, conduct research on the interview, and lead interview training sessions. He also serves as an adjunct professor in the Psychology Department at the University of Memphis.

Paul welcomes questions and comments. Feel free to contact him through **paulcgreen.com** or **medialearninginternational.com**.

PREFACE

This is a practical book on the selection interview. It is also a companion to *Actions Speak!*, an interview training video, and its parallel applications in e-learning, webinars, structured interview development, classroom instruction, and live Internet seminars.

Many readers will be first-time interviewers who want to learn how to predict performance and avoid legal problems. Others will be experienced interviewers who want to mine the book for current ideas or new understanding. Workplace trainers might use the book in their classes, or to prepare learners for e-learning, classroom training, or live Internet training. Those interested in interview research might benefit by reading *Get Talent: Interview for Actions, Select for Results*. That book is a heavier read on behavior-based interviewing, offering the research foundations of interviewing with explanations of the "why to" and "how to" of interviewing. Much of *Actions Speak!* was derived from it.

My personal approach as a writer and consultant is to help interviewers and organizations measure candidates' job skills and predict their job performance in a defensible way. At the same time, it is my goal to protect job candidates from interviewers who rely on "people skills," intuitions, free-form interviews, and personal theories of success to make selection decisions. I believe that my objectives are best achieved when I introduce practical interviewing techniques that are consistent with published research, selection law, and best practices.

The behavior-based strategy came from the research and professional practice of industrial organizational psychologists over several decades. It is also known as behavioral interviewing, behavior description interviewing, competency-based interviewing, and a variety of product names. When I first conducted interviewing seminars in the early 1980s, I was very protective of the words "Behavioral Interviewing," along with my company's registered trademark for our interviewing product. But since those days, the term has become a part of standard business language and the behavioral interviewing concept has been adapted by consultants, authors, and program developers. So I decided to adopt the term "behavior-based interviewing" and separate my thinking from some of the ideas advocated by others.

There are many words and phrases that are used to describe what is measured in the selection interview. Here are some of the most common:

- Knowledge
- Skill
- Ability
- Other characteristics
- Trait
- Competency
- Personality
- Dimension
- Factor
- Capability
- Proficiency

There is a problem here. Each of these expressions has its own meaning, which in turn can influence how you validate and defend your interviews. To address this challenge, I have elected to use the terms "skill" and "competency" to describe only what is measured by a behavior-based interview.

When I use these words I am referring to purposeful actions that can be observed, described, measured, and verified. To be more specific:

- A skill is an observable behavior or activity that leads to a desired work outcome. It may involve relatively simple actions such as working with one's hands, or a combination of actions included in activities such as negotiating, selling, and influencing.

- A behavior-based competency is a combination of observable behaviors and activities that lead to a desired work outcome. Competencies are often combined into "competency models" that can be used for selection, training, and communications. (See appendix D for a list of behavior-based competencies.)

These definitions of skill and competency are critical for understanding the real meaning of the behavior-based interviewing strategy. The mission is to observe and evaluate past actions to predict future job performance. As you will see, I will avoid using the words "ability" or "trait." Special training is typically required to assess these qualities in an interview, and most of the readers of this book will not have completed advanced studies in the behavioral sciences.

The *Actions Speak!* video, this book, and our structured interviewing tools would have never been produced without the wisdom, business experience, and skills of Art Bauer. He has produced well over 1,000 training videos and learning products over his 40-year career. He also used these skills to keep me on target and productive for our customers. Along the way, he over-communicated to ensure that we were in sync, and he tolerated my compulsive attention to detail and tendency to overwork even a simple assignment.

Finally, there is something I need to confess. This may sound a little corny, but I've had a lifetime passion for doing selection interviews. Many of these interviews were for critical jobs in management, aviation, and law enforcement. Others were for individual contributors, like bookkeepers, truck drivers, and telemarketers. Doing these interviews taught me that there were many candidates who tolerated me, colleagues who were smarter than me, and clients who grounded me in the realities of selection. These experiences helped me learn, and were sometimes painful. But they were usually beneficial.

It is my hope that *Actions Speak!* will help you learn, without the pain.

Paul C. Green, Ph.D.
Miramar Beach, Florida
January 2012

INTRODUCTION

The odds are that when you picked up this book you wanted a "no frills," quick read that would give you solid information on how to conduct a selection interview. You probably want just enough information to enable you to be a professional and effective member of a hiring team. You don't want the details of legal cases or basic research findings—just a sensible explanation of what to do, and not do, when interviewing.

That's what this book will give you. It approaches behavior-based interviewing in three parts—before the interview, during the interview, and after the interview. Each of these sections deals with both the "why to" and "how to" of interviewing. Collectively, they will help you prepare to interview, conduct a structured, behavior-based interview, and assess candidates in a reliable, defensible way.

The first part, Prepare to Measure, consists of three chapters that deal with accurate, fair measurement of candidates' job skills. Chapter 1 (Understand Behavior-Based Interviewing) explains how measurable past actions are the best predictors of future performance. In chapter 2 (Question the Intuitive Approach), you will see how first impressions, interviewing mistakes, wild-card questions, and free-form interviews interfere with measurement. Then we will explore the benefits of using a structured interview and explain how to build a structured interview that will help you measure a candidate's job skills (Chapter 3, Use a Structured Interview).

Part two, Discover with Discipline, is about using a disciplined approach to discover a candidate's job skills during the interview itself. In chapter 4 (Start with a Good Plan) you will see how to use "comfort" questions, willingness questions, career questions, knowledge questions, and competency questions. Chapter 5 (Seek Behavioral Predictors) shows how to discover examples of past actions that will help you predict future performance. Then, in chapter 6, I will explain how to "Finish with a Nimble Wrap-up," with practical tips on how to conclude the interview in a professional and respectful way.

The third part of the book, Rate and Respect, is about what happens after the interview is over. Its single chapter outlines how interviewers can evaluate the candidate's employability using a two-step process that matches answers to job-related competencies. This chapter also introduces one way to conduct a decision-making session that will involve other interviewers and stakeholders in the selection process.

Some readers only want to read the "essence" of a book. In *Actions Speak!* this would be chapter 5, Seek Behavioral Predictors. It explains how you can help a candidate describe his past actions to enable you to predict his future performance. You see how to identify the important who, what, when, where, and how of past behavior, and how to estimate the extent to which a candidate has a job skill. This is the foundation for the behavior-based strategy. I've coached thousands of people on how to gain a behavioral predictor and have found that this skill defines their effectiveness as an interviewer.

The Resources at the end of the book will give you different examples of structured interviews as well as information on federal policies regarding lawful and unlawful interview questions. Keep in mind, however, that this book is no substitute for getting competent legal advice, particularly in light of the ever-changing nature and number of federal, state, and municipal laws governing employment selection. Along this line of thinking, I must say that selection laws have raised the standards on how to do an interview. Much of today's law does not hobble interviewers; instead, it encourages the use of a disciplined, science-based approach.

As you will see, there are a lot of moving parts in an interview. This points to a practical reality: if you want to be an effective interviewer, you must give your full attention to learn how to be proficient. You can do this and be a master interviewer—if you will commit to learning the information and skills provided in *Actions Speak!*

PART ONE

BEFORE THE INTERVIEW:
PREPARE TO
MEASURE

The manager looked at me as though I had told him he was brushing his teeth all wrong.

"What do you mean, structured interview? I've worked here fifteen years. I know what everyone does, what each job involves, what kind of person is best for each position. Why would I need a crib sheet to ask the right questions when I'm interviewing a candidate?"

"Well, for one thing," I said, "do you ask every candidate for a particular job the same or very similar questions?"

"No, of course not. I just let the conversation go where it wants. Each candidate is different and brings different experience, different skills to the job. Some applicants have a lot more to say than others—but I usually know if he's a good hire within the first five minutes."

"Do you sometimes forget to ask an important question, say, about a critical job skill?"

"Rarely," he said. "I can usually fill in the blanks myself. Sometimes I can even tell by looking."

"Do you take notes?"

"Sure. I bring a pencil and pad with me."

"Do you write down exactly what the candidate says?"

"No, but I've got a good memory," he said, showing some irritation.

"And how often do you have to interview for a given position?" I asked.

"Not that often," he said flatly.

"Well," I replied, "I've taken the liberty of looking at your retention rate. Your company's turnover is nearly double the average rate in your industry. For each worker you hire at a salary of $50,000 a year, it's costing you an additional $50,000 in training costs, unemployment benefits, outplacement costs, performance degradation, and other factors. Your company hires 20 people at this pay level, and you're replacing 10 a year instead of 5. This means that you're paying an extra quarter-million dollars a year, hiring a lot of underqualified people, while fighting to stay competitive. Not only that, but you're opening yourself up to discrimination lawsuits. You haven't had any lately, but you're vulnerable because you're handling people differently. And compared to that, even if you defend yourself successfully, a quarter-million is chump change."

He just looked at me.

"You may not be aware of it," I continued, "but by letting the interview go 'wherever it wants,' and by basing skill assessment on how the candidate looks, and by relying on your memory of what the candidate said in an hour-long interview, you're letting your preconceptions dictate your hiring. And that's not defensible, no matter how fair you think you're being. You're playing with fire."

He looked at me. He looked at the lawyer at one end of the table. He looked at the CFO sitting beside him. He looked at the CEO at the other end.

He said, "Tell me what we need to do."

1

UNDERSTAND BEHAVIOR-BASED INTERVIEWING

The behavior-based interviewing strategy has become the most widely accepted method for conducting selection interviews. The basic premise is:

Past actions are the best predictors of future performance.

It's common sense. People don't change much. Typically they will behave in the future as they behaved in the past. When this logic is applied to interviewing, job candidates are asked to give descriptions of real times when they used their work skills. The interviewer then uses their responses to evaluate their skills and predict how they will perform in a new job. This approach is not perfect, but it is a reasonable way to interview.

The behavior-based strategy has emerged from the science and practice of industrial organizational psychology. The science of selection is reflected in research on effective interviewing techniques. Practitioners apply this research to improve the ways they conduct interviews. This combination of science and practice has produced interviewing techniques that are research-based, practical, and legally defensible.[1]

The behavior-based strategy has been adapted by managers, consultants, and trainers to meet their special circumstances. But even though there are variations in their approaches, they share the idea that past behavior predicts future behavior. In addition, the most effective and defensible approaches will emphasize using a structured interview guide, treating all candidates in an equivalent way, and asking job-related questions.

WHAT IS A BEHAVIOR?

A behavior can be observed, measured and verified. You can see or hear a behavior when it occurs, just as you can see or hear a skill that is being used. This makes it more likely that behavior-based interviewers can build consensus on a candidate's qualifications.

With the behavior-based strategy, the interviewer asks job-related, past-event questions about things that the candidate did in prior work situations. She then helps the candidate give examples of past actions and uses them to measure job skills and predict job performance. When this approach is used in a disciplined way, better candidates are hired, skills are matched to job requirements, and legal liability is minimized. There is a real payoff in using a systematic approach to measure job skills and select the right person for the job.

Interviewers are encouraged to be objective in the ways they gather and interpret information. This means avoiding first impressions, candidate stereotyping, and hiring someone "like me." Rather, the interviewer is expected to collect information about past actions, follow the structured interview guide, and take notes that describe what was done in a particular situation. Answers are evaluated by comparing examples of past work to the

WHERE DID BEHAVIOR-BASED INTERVIEWING COME FROM?

No single person invented the behavior-based interviewing strategy. It came from the research and professional practice of industrial organizational psychologists over several decades. Much of this work has been associated with job analysis, development of structured interviews, applying a systematic interviewing system, adapting to legal standards, and interview validation.

ASK OPEN-ENDED, SINGULAR, PAST-EVENT QUESTIONS

It is not unusual for interviewers to ask the following question:

"Tell me, what are your strengths?"

It is also typical to hear an answer something like this:

"I am a 'people person' who enjoys working with others. I am a good problem-solver, based on what others say. And I feel that I am very organized."

But there is a problem here. A general question about "strengths" invites the candidate to give a smooth sales pitch. The solution is to ask a past-event question that will lead the candidate to give an example of a specific thing that was done at work. Generalities are pleasant, but specifics predict.

---

skills and competencies needed to do the job well. With the behavior-based strategy, evaluation is a process, not a general intuition or snap judgment.

A behavior-based interviewer will always ask questions from a written list of questions that were designed for the specific job to be filled. Often structured interviews have questions organized under competencies and offer a way to rate or evaluate answers. Generally, the interviewer has some flexibility about which questions to ask. But in some cases the interviewer is required to read all questions to candidates, in order, and with no allowance for probing.

USE A JOB-RELATED, STRUCTURED INTERVIEW

A structured interview is a written list of questions to ask in your interview. In part B of the Resources at the end of this book you will find an example of a structured interview for a workforce recruiter, including four questions for each of the competencies to be assessed, rating boxes to use in evaluating the candidate's answers, and space to write notes.

Defensible and effective interview questions come from a job analysis and are specifically designed for the job you want to fill. It may be tempting to pull a list of questions from your file, but the most effective questions are a reflection of what needs to be done on a particular job. Often interview questions are built from the job tasks in a job description or competencies. This way each question on the structured interview can be traced back to job requirements.

There are a few critical steps to take when creating a structured interview:

1. Conduct a job-analysis for the target job and build a list of job tasks.
2. Create a job description that lists 30 or more important job tasks and other requirements for the position. (If you already have an up-to-date job description and job analysis, much of this work will already have been done for you.)
3. Meet with job experts to develop competencies[2] and organize the most important tasks under them.
4. Have the job experts select the most important job tasks and convert them into meaningful questions for a structured interview.

The job experts are a critical part of this process. They have strong knowledge of what skills and competencies the job will require. Typically, they have done the job themselves, have conducted a job analysis, or have managed people who perform the job. This gives them a unique perspective in identifying exactly what the person will need to do in the job and in creating questions to measure their skills.

WHAT IS A COMPETENCY?

Competencies are descriptions of job skills or working habits that an employee needs in order to be effective in a particular job or to fit into an organization. They are used to organize interview questions and to help you evaluate a candidate's answers. Competencies are listed in part D of the Resources section.

It may seem that creating structured interviews is too time consuming—but the biggest time consumer is working with someone who can't or won't do the job. Once an interview is created it can be used until the job changes significantly. Imagine that your organization has prepared structured interviews for every job in your organization. This means that

- the interviews are ready for use at a moment's notice,
- all interviewers know exactly what to ask, and
- training can focus how to use specific interviews.

The short-term investment in time required to create a structured interview yields long-term benefits.

STANDARD QUESTIONS VERSUS PAST-EVENT QUESTIONS

Standard	Past Event
"What are your goals?"	"What is your primary goal and what did you do to achieve it last year?"
"To what extent are you work motivated?"	"Describe a project that reflects on your work motivation."
"Tell me about your skills in creativity and innovation."	"Give me an example of a time when you were creative."
"What is your philosophy on work-life balance?"	"Tell me about a specific time when you followed your values on work-life balance."
"What is your primary strength on the job?"	"Describe a time when your number-one strength got results on the job."

ASK PAST-EVENT QUESTIONS

The purpose of asking past-event questions (often called "behavioral" questions) is to help the candidate describe his past behavior in a work situation. Research has shown that past-event questions are effective in getting information that will predict job performance. For example, compare these questions:

Typical question: "Describe your leadership style for me."

Past-event question: "Tell me about a leadership challenge you experienced at work. What was the situation and what did you do?"

It is very important to word past-event (behavioral) questions to reflect job requirements. Ideally, this is accomplished by converting job tasks or activities into questions. Also, past-event questions are always worded in singular, as opposed to plural, terms. Ask about "a time when," not "times when." This will help communicate that you want to hear about a specific thing the candidate did.

> To predict what the person will do, first measure what the person has done.

SEEK BEHAVIORAL PREDICTORS

A behavioral predictor is the candidate's description of what was done in an actual place, in real time, when performing a particular task. It is more than just a routine action, like arriving at work or following directions. It is a jewel of information that is a meaningful sample of past behavior. This is the foundation of the behavior-based interviewing strategy: it provides information on a past action that will help the interviewer predict job performance.

Behavioral predictors don't always appear spontaneously in an interview. Sometimes, even with well-written questions, you will have to help the candidate (1) recall a time when she used her skills and (2) describe specifically what she did. Not every candidate finds it easy to answer a series of past-event questions. Here are two ways you can help:

- Keep silent while the candidate is thinking of an answer. Silence is your friend. If you interrupt the candidate's thinking, you may be shutting down a revealing answer—so be quiet and wait for the answer.

- Redirect an answer. When the candidate is giving you generalities or self-promotion, it makes sense to redirect the conversation. Politely interrupt and move to the next question. Then he will stop talking, listen, and respond.

You also have to recognize when you are getting a generality instead of a behavioral predictor. For example, look at this answer:

"Let's see . . . okay . . . once I had a job where the manual filing system was frequently out of control, because people would usually just get a file without checking it out. If they did return it they would typically just toss it in a stack. It started to drive me crazy. It wasn't really part of my job, but I took on the job of dealing with the problem."

The words "frequently," "usually," "if," and "typically" in her response suggest that the candidate is giving a general answer that will not predict job performance. So, instead of accepting a vague response, the interviewer has the opportunity to probe and draw out a behavioral predictor. For example:

"What specific actions did you take? What did you do to reorganize the system, to get things running smoothly?"

With this type of follow-up question, you are likely to get specifics on the "who," "when," "what," "where," and "how" of the solution:

"Well, I worked to almost 10:00 that night. First, I isolated all the duplicate files that could be consolidated. Second, I set up a checkout system, so we knew specifically where all these valuable paper files were at all times. Third, I made a full count on the core files. Fourth, I. . . ."

It is possible to gain a behavioral predictor well over 90 percent of the time that you ask a past-event question. An efficient interviewer can get at least one behavioral predictor every 2½ minutes. This means that you can gather 10 to 20 behavioral predictors every time you interview.

Just one more point here. When you ask a past-event question you will typically see the candidate look away briefly. The break in eye contact is a practical signal that she is trying to think of an answer. This is a cue for you to wait. Be silent. Don't jump to the conclusion that the person has a weak character or is fabricating an answer; just stay silent and listen for specifics that will reflect on the candidate's job skills.

Present questions in a conversational tone to communicate exactly what you need to know.

PROBE BASED ON NON-VERBAL SIGNALS

Even though you ask effective job-related questions and probe into the answer, you will sense that there are times when the answer is not complete. When you do, you may choose to follow non-verbal signals, or "feeling clues," that reflect the emotions involved in a behavioral predictor.

None of us are mind readers when it comes to knowing how another person really feels, but all of us can learn to recognize the non-verbal indicators of feelings. Things like a facial expression, hand gesture, or body shift can signal that there's more to the answer than you are hearing. This is especially important when a non-verbal signal doesn't match the answer. When this happens, ask a behavioral probe to get more information.

The most practical way for me to advise you on this is to say that you can see when a person is giving an indication of comfort or discomfort with an answer. There is no formula for what type of behavior to look for. You have to look at the person while talking and make a judgment if there is a positive or negative feeling associated with the answer.

Sometimes a body shift means eagerness, at other times disappointment. A hand gesture may reflect confidence, but in other cases it can indicate nervousness. Much of what a non-verbal signal means is based on the situation, the person's typical way of self-expression, or the intensity of the gesture. You have to look at the person and gauge whether the non-verbal behavior matches the verbal behavior in the answer.

Let's assume you asked a candidate how he maintained his technical knowledge. But you hear a general answer, along with a change in his voice, posture, and gestures that told you there were some negative feelings embedded in the answer. So you ask a job-related, behavioral probe:

> "Please tell me specifically what you did to stay up to date, particularly with regard to taking classes."

Notice that this is not a question about feelings. Don't play psychologist, psychiatrist, or counselor. This question is about taking classes. It was prompted by non-verbal signals that the candidate felt discomfort involving technical knowledge.

> Probe for more information when a non-verbal signal indicates either a strong positive or negative feeling.

You can get valuable information by responding to non-verbal signals by asking job-related probes. Instead of harboring a vague intuition that something is not right with the answer, ask a probe to gain more information. It does not always yield valuable information, but over time your efforts will help you get a representative sample of the candidate's skills, negative and positive.

ASK REVERSE QUESTIONS

When you get an answer with strong positive or negative information, ask a reverse question to test your understanding. There are several reasons why this is important. You may have

- confirmed your first impression,
- overweighed negative information,
- been guilty of the "like me" syndrome, or
- stereotyped the candidate.

As a result, you may see a negative or a positive where it doesn't exist.

You can also have a biased perspective for the highly qualified candidate. When the candidate has the exact work experience and education you need, you might forget to look for negative information. For example, a top new hire could have fantastic skills in manufacturing, cost accounting, and information technology—but you can be so impressed that you forget to ask questions about leadership and teamwork. In other words, your positive bias can cause you to not look for negatives.

REVERSE QUESTIONS

You can reverse the direction of a question by changing a few words.

Positive Question	Reverse Question
"When were you recognized as an effective team member?"	"When were you given negative feedback on your team skills?"
"Describe an important goal you set in your last job. What did you achieve?"	"What goal did you set in your last job but did not achieve?"
"When did your leadership skills enable you to get strong results?"	"Tell me about a time when your leadership skills failed you."
"How did your flexibility help you work effectively with an irrational customer?"	"When were you too flexible with an irrational customer? What happened?"

Another reason why it is important to ask reverse questions is that every positive can become a negative if taken to an extreme.

- Motivation . . . can turn you into a workaholic.
- Organization . . . can make you obsessive-compulsive.
- Teamwork . . . can make you too dependent.
- Creativity . . . can lead you to be impractical.
- Extraversion . . . can interfere with being a good listener.

Similarly, every weakness can be the foundation for building new, positive habits.

- The workaholic . . . learns how to balance work and family.
- The obsessive-compulsive . . . learns how to tolerate ambiguity.
- The non-asserter . . . learns how to make a request.
- The impractical person . . . learns to test ideas.
- The poor listener . . . learns active listening skills.

The practical conclusion is that not all positives are great and not all negatives are horrible. Ask reverse questions to get a representative sample of a broad spectrum of the candidate's experiences.

Snap judgments, stereotyping, and bias can keep qualified candidates out of jobs and put unqualified ones in them.

INTERVIEWING FOR PERSONAL QUALITIES

Interviewers who embrace the behavioral strategy are often cautious about using the interview to assess personality traits such as integrity, honesty, and values. This is because the behavioral approach is less theoretical, more trainable, easily adapted, and reasonably defensible. Also, few interviewers have the professional training needed to reliably assess personality traits. In most situations today, it is more practical for interviewers to assess behaviors.

However, we tend to talk about people in terms of their traits, not their behaviors. Consider a bank teller. It is legitimate for a manager and co-workers to expect the teller to be honest (a trait), particularly with financial transactions. What about an airline pilot? Don't you want your pilot to be conscientious (a trait) about reading the instruments in the cockpit, rather than being distracted by the copilot's comments about company policies?

There is the added question of how to assess whether the candidate has personal qualities that fit the work culture. The concept of culture fit is often expressed as shared values, opinions, and beliefs, not as behaviors. For example, it is easy to recognize that things move more smoothly when a co-worker shares an understanding of the job and organizational context.

- An EEOC litigator will probably perform better if she buys into the values and mission of the agency.

- A software engineer will probably be more effective if his opinions align with the policies and procedures of his employer.

- A police officer may be safer if she believes that in some circumstances the use of deadly force is justified.

But even if you build reasonable, job-related questions based on work culture, there can be questions of legality when interviewing for values, opinions, and beliefs. You certainly don't want to move into prohibited topics about religion, family, bankruptcy, lifestyle, and other personal choices. Just think, how would you feel about being assessed by an interviewer on your personal values about marriage, religion, or politics?

One solution is to take special care in applying the behavioral approach. For example, you could build your interviewing strategy on a job analysis. Determine what people really need to do in order to be effective. Then turn the job requirements into interview questions.

GIVE RESPECT AND SHOW VALUES

Behavior-based interviewing is a powerful tool for predicting job performance, but this approach will also reveal the person behind the skills. Sometimes candidates will share personal concerns like fears, disappointments, dreams, and failures. When this happens, you may be tempted to be an efficient interviewer—ignore feelings, interrupt the candidate, ask another question, and wait for the answer.

But sometimes it is better to be an inefficient interviewer. Put down your pen and listen. Show respect for the person behind the words. Take the time needed to understand what is important to the candidate. See more than the candidate's job skills and recognize the candidate as a person, rather than just a bundle of skills in a nice suit.

Another approach is to convert a personal quality into a behavioral question. Here are some behavioral questions involving honesty:

"When you were honest even though it was embarrassing for you? What did you say?"

"Describe a time when you accurately reported on your performance, even when it made you look bad."

"Tell me about a time when you were tough-minded about telling the truth."

"Describe a situation when you saw a colleague fudge information in a report. What did you do?"

The conclusion? You can measure personal qualities while avoiding legal difficulties by skillfully converting important job behaviors into interview questions.

SUMMARY

The behavior-based interviewing strategy is based on the idea that past actions are the best predictors of job performance. This is the foundation for behavior-based interviewing—discover what a person has done in order to predict what he will do. However, there are challenges in applying this concept. Interviewers are often guilty of using snap judgments, selecting "like me" candidates, asking the wrong questions, or accepting a candidate's promotional answers.

You can minimize interviewing errors through the use of a job-related structured interview with questions organized under competencies. An effective interviewer will comfortably present structured interview questions, gain behavioral predictors, and use past actions to predict job performance. Research has shown that this approach is reliable, valid, and defensible. And, if you take time to really listen, you will be able to combine effective prediction with respect for the person.

CHAPTER 2

QUESTION THE INTUITIVE APPROACH

What is your interviewing approach really like?

Do you think of yourself as an intuitive, free-form interviewer who can "size up" people based on your life experiences? Are you one of those people who have "street smarts" about job candidates? Perhaps you feel that you can "read" people because of what you have learned in competitive sports, academics, or business.

Or would you say that your approach is more disciplined and behavior based? Do you ask questions from a structured interview form, gain behavioral predictors, and ask reverse questions? Are you more interested in discovering the candidate's job skills than exploring his personality traits? What about evaluating answers? Do you use rating anchors to compare answers to job requirements?

These choices represent two opposite approaches used by interviewers today. Obviously, I advocate the behavior-based strategy. I also know from experience that many interviewers feel good about using a more intuitive, relaxed approach. But this comfort zone can become a danger zone if the interviewer's approach interferes with accurate measurement of a candidate's job skills.

I'm not going to say that all intuitive interviewers are ineffective. Some people do have unique experiences that they can use to help them assess candidates. But these people are rare. Besides, it would not be fun to go to court and explain why you consider your intuitions superior to research-based interviewing techniques. It is better to question the intuitive approach rather than adopt it blindly.

In this chapter we will begin with a look at ways that first impressions, stereotypes, and snap judgments can interfere with your effectiveness. Next, we will talk about your "improvables," or interviewing mistakes that reduce the accuracy of your interview findings. Then we will continue with the problems that come from asking "wild-card" questions, conducting a free-form interview, and allowing bias to influence your interviewing. Finally, we will explore how interviewing science and structured interviewing can work for you.

The driving concept behind all of this discussion is that effective interviewing means good measurement. Reliable, accurate measurement is the foundation for valid prediction.

WHAT ABOUT YOUR FIRST IMPRESSIONS?

Sure, you have first impressions of people. We all have them. But where do they come from, and why do you react positively to some people and negatively to others?

There is no magic to sensing what another person is like. Instead, your first impression of a person you meet today is influenced by the people you have known in your past. For example, you could have a negative reaction to a candidate because he reminds you of

- a pushy ad man,
- your ex-spouse's father,
- the last person you fired,
- a criminal you saw on TV, or
- the worker who kicked your dog.

The same goes for a positive first impression. The candidate you really like could remind you of your favorite aunt or the stockbroker who made you a ton of money.

Of course, it's more convenient to assume you have an "inner wisdom" about people. But the first few minutes of any interview will only afford you an opportunity to meet the candidate and build rapport. It will not give you enough information to make an effective hiring decision.

First impressions tend to shut down the process of getting information about skills. Imagine that you interview a candidate with a top-of-the-line résumé, Hollywood good looks, and a positive attitude. It's understandable that you would have a positive reaction to this person—but all you really know is that he can make a good impression. Instead of jumping to a decision, you need to move ahead and gain information about his actual job skills.

> The content of a candidate's answer is king; the impressions you have of him are suspect.

Stereotyping works in a similar way, but it involves popular beliefs and assumptions about groups of people. These assumptions can blind the interviewer to a candidate's true skills and interfere with accurate assessment of job skills and qualifications. In addition, many stereotypes are associated with illegal factors in employment such as gender, race, color, religion, national origin, age, disabilities, or personal preferences.

The interviewer who is influenced by first impressions and stereotypes is prone to make snap judgments and decide a candidate's future based on subjective feelings. It makes better sense to use the behavior-based approach to gather information about job skills, then make a decision based on reliable information about the candidate's qualifications.

CONSIDER YOUR "IMPROVABLES"

When you take a close look at your approach to interviewing, the odds are you'll discover room for improvement. Self-examination will help you spot

A GHOST FROM THE PAST

I once had a powerful, negative first impression of a candidate. When I examined my feelings, I realized that she reminded me of a grade school teacher who hit me with a ruler whenever I made a mistake. Once I understood the cause of my reaction, I put extra effort into getting information on the candidate's job skills. My teacher was the actual cause of my negative intuition. It would not have been fair to penalize the candidate based on my reaction to someone else's bad behavior.

the mistakes you tend to make as an interviewer—commonsense things such as not building rapport or cutting the interview short. There are also less obvious errors like having vague selection criteria or being guilty of the "halo effect." When you minimize the mistakes that you make, you are more likely to do a good job in measuring the candidate's skills.

On the following pages you will find a list of interviewing mistakes to look over. It was based on research and observations of several thousand people doing interviews in classes. I concluded that there were four major types of interview mistakes:

- Poor relationship management, including poor rapport building and unprofessional comments
- Unreliable measurement practices, such as cutting interviews short or not planning the interview
- Making errors in interview administration, ranging from starting late through giving clues on how to answer
- Committing evaluation errors, including the use of vague selection criteria and doing global ratings of interview performance

When you make these types of mistakes, you are reducing the measurement effectiveness of the interview. For example, if you ask a closed-ended question that asks for a yes or no response, you are less likely to get a full and complete answer. Less information means lower accuracy in your interview ratings.

Think of your interviewing mistakes as being "improvables" that suggest learning opportunities. After each interview, ask yourself, "What did I do, and what did I not do, that would have improved my assessment of this person?" The new skills that you learn will build your confidence and professionalism as an interviewer.

Look at the list of improvables on the following pages to see what types of mistakes you make and how you can learn from them. Then continue with the next section. You will learn to avoid "wild-card" questions, reject the free-form interview, and benefit from the science of interviewing.

AVOID WILD-CARD QUESTIONS

It can be fun to ask some of your favorite off-the-wall questions. When you are clever with them, the interview is dynamic, the candidate reveals

Improvables	Problem	Solution
Poor Relationship Management		
Lack of rapport building	Candidate anxiety can interfere with giving complete answers.	Smile and get the candidate talking by asking casual, opener questions.
Unprofessional comments	The interviewer may lose credibility and limit information flow.	Avoid profanity, ethnic jokes and comments, and protected topics; use conventional language.
Unreliable Measurement		
Cutting the interview short	Information is missed and measurement is inconsistent.	Keep interviews equivalent for all candidates for the same job.
Using a free-form interview	Results affected by overtalking, lack of focus, digression, low reliability.	Ask questions from a job-related, structured interview.
Errors in Administration		
Starting late, ending early	Candidates for the same job are not treated equivalently.	Estimate how long interviews need to be before conducting them; begin and end on time.
Closed-ended questions	Short answers limit the information available for selection.	Ask questions that require an informative answer. Minimize questions that can be answered yes or no.
Talking too much	Overtalking by the interviewer limits discovery.	Permit silence so the candidate can think and respond.
Inefficient questioning	Speculative, strange, or illegal questions limit information flow.	Do a job analysis to develop a structured interview with job-related questions.
Inconsistent questioning	Easy questions are asked of some, difficult questions of others.	Ask the same questions or similar questions of all candidates.
Forgetting answers	It is impossible to remember everything a candidate says.	Take notes that paraphrase or quote the candidate's exact language.
Failure to listen	Key words and patterns of information will be lost.	Take notes to ensure attention and document the candidate's answer.
Irritating habits	The interviewer may distract the candidate with personal habits.	Discover your irritating mannerisms and replace them with new habits.
Accepting a candidate's self-promotion	Failure to get specific information on the candidate's skills.	Ask specific questions about particular situations or past events.
Signaling evaluation of an answer	A reaction to an answer may influence the candidate's response.	Avoid smiles, nods, comments that clue the candidate on how answers are evaluated.

Improvables	Problem	Solution
Errors in Evaluating Answers		
Unclear selection criteria	There is no standard for evaluating answers or probing.	Write selection objectives as competencies, experience, or educational standards.
Overweighing negatives	Negative information impacts interview ratings more than positives.	Ask reverse questions that sample positive and negative information.
Snap judgments	A quick decision is based on stereotypes, personal reactions, or appearance.	Postpone decision making until answers are evaluated.
The "halo" effect	A high rating on one skill disposes high ratings on other skills.	Use a systematic approach to read over each skill and rate each separately.
The "like me" effect	Ratings are influenced by similarity of candidate and interviewer.	Rate a candidate's skills by comparing notes with written selection standards.
Stereotyping	The assumed qualities of a group are applied to an individual.	Use rating anchors to compare a candidate's skills with prewritten selection criteria.
Personal success theory	Evaluation is based on a theory of success that is not validated.	Compare an individual's qualities with competencies and selection criteria.
First impression overhang	First impressions influence the way the interview is done.	Conduct each interview in a standard way to accurately sample information.
Intuitive selection	Feelings are a less reliable predictor of performance than information.	Ask reverse questions to generate information that may disprove intuitions.
The contrast effect	Comparing people with people is unfair because the standard is variable.	Rate a skill, not a person, by comparing interview notes with selection standards.
Global rating	One overall rating does not account for highs and lows in a person's skills.	Develop a profile of skills by comparing interview notes with separate competencies.

personal secrets, and you can feel empowered. With so much energy around these questions, you just have to get a little buzz. After all, you think, who wants to be bored in an interview?

But the hard fact is that you are not conducting an interview for entertainment purposes. Your job as an interviewer is to determine whether a person can do a particular job well. You are not there to test your own theories, discover secrets, or stress the candidate. Effective questions enable you to get information that you can use to predict job performance.

The best way to evaluate questions is to determine whether the question links directly to what the person is expected to do on the job. Write questions that link to important job tasks. Make the linkage obvious. For example, if the job requires using project management software, ask questions about using software.

Wild-card questions are not the best choice for gaining behavioral information. They may be effective in a singles bar, in getting people to laugh, or in getting attention in a speech. But for an interview they can be insensitive, useless, and indefensible. Effective questions are job-related, have face validity, and get you information that can predict job performance.

THERE IS NO PERFECT INTERVIEW

The goal is to do better interviews, not perfect interviews. Every interview can teach you how to minimize mistakes so you can improve your accuracy in measuring a candidate's skills.

There is an additional concern. Questions that encourage speculation by the candidate can be more of an opportunity for self-promotion than

---

WILD-CARD QUESTIONS

Find the one good question among the following:

"What is your philosophy of success?"

"Where do you come from?"

"How does a bird fly?"

"How many children do you have?"

"If you were a skunk, how would you smell the roses?"

"Did you know that the last guy I hired lasted six hours?"

"Prove to me why should I hire you."

"What did you learn in church last week?"

"How rich do you want to be?"

"What specific thing did you do last year to close a big sale?"

The correct choice is on the next page.

a tool for getting behavioral predictors. Consider the question, "What is your philosophy of success?" Then reflect on the likely answer—a glowing description of positive traits like honesty, persistence, and flexibility. When you invite the candidate to sell you on her skills, you spend time hearing self-promotion rather than discovering what she actually can do.

REJECT THE FREE-FORM INTERVIEW

As you saw on the list of improvables, there are many things to learn. But there is one improvable so significant that I have to say it is critical. It is the most important thing an interviewer can do, and it is ignored by a substantial number of today's interviewers. You must use a structured approach rather than a free-form interview. (For examples of structured interviews, see parts B and C in the Resources section.)

The free-form interview has no list of questions, no place for notes, and no guidance on evaluating answers. The emphasis is on spontaneity, flow, and general impressions. Questions are asked as they come to the mind of the interviewer, and candidates tend to be evaluated on their social skills and likability. The result is unreliable measurement of the candidate's job skills. If you don't measure effectively, you can't predict effectively.

At best, the free-form interview will produce general impressions rather than specific information. This is a major limitation, because professional rating systems require the interviewer to rate or score a candidate's responses to questions. If the interviewer does not get specific information, then it is very difficult to rate the candidate's true skills and competencies.

A free-form interview is less likely to survive legal scrutiny than a structured interview. Since it is based on the interviewer's preferences, it does not meet the professional standards for being a job-related interview. In addition, candidates are treated differently because they are asked different questions.

WHAT IS A GOOD QUESTION?

Good questions evoke information on the candidate's skills that will predict job performance. Of the questions listed on the previous page, the only one that meets this criterion is "What specific thing did you do last year to close a big sale?" This type of question doesn't invite speculation, sound strange, or relate to race, gender, color, national origin, age, disabilities, or lifestyle.

INTERVIEW STRUCTURE AND CHEMISTRY

Good chemistry between the interviewer and candidate does not ensure strong performance on the job—nor does bad interview chemistry ensure poor job performance. The practical thing to do is to use your structured interview to get information that will predict job performance. Chemistry is nice, but information predicts.

It is easy for the free-form interviewer to slip into conversation that links to race, gender, religion, color, national origin, age, disabilities, lifestyle, or other prohibited topics. I am reminded of a class participant who told me that he didn't intend to be sexist when he asked about a female candidate's family. A fellow student commented, "Your intentions don't matter. The real question is, what did the candidate think you meant?"

A structured interview is a confidence builder. It reflects a clear understanding of what needs to be done in the job. There is a list of defensible questions to ask in order to see if the candidate can do the job. The combination of clarity and good questions will help the interviewer feel confident and advance the image of the organization in the eyes of the candidate.

BENEFIT FROM THE SCIENCE OF INTERVIEWING

Over the past 65 years research review articles and commentaries by experts point to one standing principle: you have to use a structured interview to get a reliable measurement of a job candidate's skills. This pattern of findings is so consistent that most experts agree that a structured approach is a critical component of effective interviewing.[3]

Although you have leeway in deciding how much structure you want in your interviews, some level of structure is essential for reliable measurement of a candidate's skills and valid prediction of performance. Interview structure also helps you manage your reactions to a candidate and helps you be confident, objective, and professional.

SUMMARY

When it comes to interviewing, perception is not reality. Yes, you do have valid experiences that have taught you a lot about people, but your perceptions of a job candidate are not enough to predict job performance. You must have the right foundation to build on. This begins with going beyond first impressions, stereotypes, snap decisions, wild-card questions, and free-form interviews. It is better to gain relevant, behavioral information to predict job performance.

CHAPTER 3

USE A STRUCTURED INTERVIEW

Shocking!

That was my thought, my reaction to the executive's comment. He was leaving our meeting to interview a new sales manager. I asked him if he was using a structured interview. He said:

"Paul, I know I should be prepared and have all the questions planned out. But this is a new job and we don't know exactly what the position will involve."

I thought, How could a successful entrepreneur not prepare to interview? Then the answer came to me. He did not believe it was important to use a structured interview.

He would have used a structured approach if he had really understood that it is

- critical for reliable measurement of job skills,
- a question guide that will ensure thoroughness,
- an indication of professionalism,
- important for defending selection decisions, and
- essential in reliably evaluating a candidate's answers.

I suspect he felt that structured interviewing was nice to do, but not really that important. He was like a carpenter going to work without a tape measure, confident that he could estimate how much to cut the materials. This chapter is written to help you understand why it is important to use a structured interview. As you read, I want you to remember that it's easy not to adopt an idea that takes effort to apply. But it is good to engage with an idea and then decide how you want to use it.

Before we move ahead, please review the structured interviews in appendices B and C. This time, ask yourself if you believe that these interviews could be helpful if you were trying to fill those jobs. What if you had structured interviews for all the jobs you fill? That would be beneficial, wouldn't it?

STRUCTURE NOW, BENEFIT LATER

The reliability of your interview findings is influenced by interview structure. If you do not use a structured approach, you will be less able to accurately measure a candidate's competencies and skills for a job. A structured interview will also help you avoid making mistakes in administering the interview (see the table of improvables in chapter 2). A pre-planned, job-related list of questions will help you discover what you need to know, avoid inappropriate questions and comments, and treat all candidates similarly.

At its most basic level, a structured approach to interviewing involves asking prepared, job-related questions of job candidates. There may be variations in the types of questions asked, how closely they link to a specific job, and what types of guidelines are given for evaluating answers. For example, structured interviews typically give the interviewer discretion as to what questions to ask or whether probing is allowed. Highly structured interviews, by contrast,

THE INTERVIEW IS A YARDSTICK

If you were installing carpet, you would need to measure the dimensions of the room. The most precise measure would be a laser ruler, followed by a tape measure, a yardstick, a 12-inch ruler, and finally, pacing it off. Each has a different level of measurement effectiveness. You would never consider just estimating the area and making a purchase. The same goes for interviewing. An eyeball estimate is not enough; the standard for measuring a candidate's skills is a structured approach with evaluation guidelines.

require that *every* question be read to the candidate, and they do not allow follow-up probes.

Whichever approach you use, you will derive multiple benefits from adopting a structured, behavior-based interview strategy. It will help you feel confident, improve retention, increase performance, and minimize liability.

Feel confident. There's a lot riding on every interview you do. The risk is that one hiring mistake can cost thousands in poor performance and lead to one hassle after another. The reward is that one hiring success can generate thousands in high performance and make life easy for you. Risk makes you cautious; reward makes you hopeful.

Over the years I found that having a structured interview gave me confidence. Job-related questions helped me feel I was effective with my phrasing. I felt that I was being fair by treating all candidates comparably. Most of all, I avoided asking off-the-wall questions that didn't link to the job. I had a solid foundation for balancing risk and reward.

STRUCTURED INTERVIEWS ARE GOAL ORIENTED

Effective managers tend to agree that setting goals improves task performance. A structured interview takes advantage of this knowledge because questions and competencies are based on specific job tasks and goals. A structured interview supports your performance as an interviewer.

My confidence was tested over and over again by candidates, employers, attorneys, and human resource managers. Most of these experiences caused me discomfort, but I always fell back on my professional values. If I committed to using a structured approach, delivered with respect, then I would get confidence, security, and a good night's sleep. Beyond these good feelings, I would hire capable performers.

New challenges to confidence come from the diversification of our workforce. Many of the candidates you interview will come from backgrounds that are very different from yours. We can expect to see continued growth in the Asian, Hispanic, and African American groups. Non-Hispanic whites will continue to be the largest single group in the workforce. However, their percentage of the workforce will continue to fall.

A structured approach will help you feel confident and comfortable interviewing diverse people. Research repeatedly says that the best strategy to use is a job-related, structured approach that is administered in a reasonably consistent way. When you have this level of preparation behind you, your confidence will grow, along with your ability to pick the right person for the job.

Improve retention. It is valuable to have a stable workforce of people who know their jobs and perform well. At one time this was described as a need to reduce turnover, but today it's more common to hear about increasing employee retention through the assessment and management of talent. This is now a critical agenda for human resource management in any organization.

Effective interviews can raise the retention rates of good workers and minimize the costs of turnover. Just think of a hiring mistake that you had to work with. What was the cost of lower performance, extra training, and stress? Consider the replacement costs, such as recruiting, travel, interview time, training a new hire, and part-time staffing—not to mention the enormous cost of replacing the critical talents and skills of a departing performer. Structured interviews will help you minimize these problems.

An Internet search on the words "turnover" and "costs" yields a broad range of estimates, but for our purposes, I will suggest that it typically costs 150–200 percent of salary and benefits to replace a manager. It costs less

---

WHAT'S THE COST OF LOSING TALENT?

Turnover can be very expensive. Here's an estimate of the average expense of losing a performer earning $80,000 a year.

Factor	% of Salary	Est. Cost
De-hiring or outplacement	10%	$ 8,000
Continued benefits or unemployment	30%	24,000
Recruiting a replacement	20%	16,000
Hiring a replacement	20%	16,000
New-hire orientation and training	20%	16,000
Legal fees or consulting	10%	8,000
Stress on the manager	5%	4,000
Losing specialized job knowledge	30%	24,000
Performance loss	20%	16,000
Reduced manpower reserves	30%	24,000
Estimated total cost:		**$156,000**

In the case of an executive, scientist, or key performer, the estimate would be considerably higher.

to lose an hourly employee, but the volume can be a killer. For example, the cost of 75 percent of the annual salary of a person making $30,000 a year is $22,500. But if you replace 100 hourly workers a year, the cost is $2,250,000. The high cost of turnover and low retention can take a huge bite out of profits. Effective interviewing can reduce these costs substantially.

Improve performance. Over time you can expect to improve overall performance by hiring more skilled people. Although work situations and recruiting opportunities differ, a substantial amount of research shows that structured interviews are effective in delivering performance benefits.

The benefits of hiring top performers are not the same for different types of work. You can expect some performance improvement for routine work and substantial improvement for highly complex work. For example, it is estimated that effective selection can provide some overall improvement of performance of hourly workers, more improvement for jobs requiring skills training or decision making, and significant improvement for jobs involving high levels of interpersonal skill or abstract reasoning.[4]

PROMOTION MISTAKES LOWER PERFORMANCE

Can you think of someone who was promoted based on likeability but couldn't do the job? How expensive was that mistake? How many benefits would have come from a good hire?

Ask yourself these questions:

- What would things be like if every job in my organization were staffed by a top performer? How much more productive would we be?

- How much could we reduce costs if we didn't have to fix mistakes? Would less time be spent dealing with personnel problems? Would it be easier to recruit? Could we get results with fewer managers?

PAY NOW—OR PAY LATER!

There's an old saying: "Pay now, or pay later. Just know you are going to pay." A disciplined approach to interviewing requires effort. You have to define competencies, train interviewers, develop structured interviews, and give equivalent treatment. But the cost is much bigger when you hire problem employees who underperform and make you pay, and pay, and pay! The one-time cost of getting ready to hire is minor compared with getting ready to fire.

Even small improvements in selection can generate substantial results. Disciplined, structured interviews will help get you there.

Minimize liability. There are many ways that personal biases can interfere with effective measurement. Most interviewers are aware of the core biases such as sexism, racism, and ageism. However, in the recent years research has defined new biases such as "weightism," and "beautism." Bias is everywhere, and it is important to be aware of your own biases and manage them.

For some time people have thought of interview bias in terms of types of questions that they ask.[5] (See appendix A for a review of protected questions and comments.) However, bias runs much deeper that the types of questions you ask. All interviewers make subtle assumptions about candidates that can influence their decisions about them.

Structured interviews appear to minimize bias. A study of judges' rulings between 1972 and 1995 in 99 federal district court cases involving discrimination in an employment interview showed that many of the components of interview structure enhanced interview reliability and validity, and thereby contributed to successful defense in litigation.[6] Objective, job-related interviews, with specific criteria, trained interviewers, and validation evidence, were largely upheld. It was also beneficial to have standardized administration, with guidelines for the interviewers, minimal discretion on questioning, common questions, and consistency. There were mixed results on the benefits of using multiple interviewers, panel interviews, and decision review.

AVOID HIGH-RISK QUESTIONS

You can reduce your risk by avoiding questions that can be linked to race, color, gender, religion, national origin, age, or disabilities. Low-risk questions can be directly related to doing a particular job.

We also need to recognize that illegal bias can often be traced to a work culture that accepts prejudicial comments. How would you expect a candidate to react to these observations?

- There was no diversity among the interviewers.
- A joke was told about religious beliefs.
- An employee was referred to as "Pop."
- There were no women in senior management.
- A disrespectful nickname was used for a disabled individual.

Bias can go unquestioned in a work climate that tolerates an undercurrent of prejudgments and unfounded assumptions about people. But bias can be minimized by insisting that interviewers be trained to use a job-related, structured interview.

BUILD A STRUCTURED INTERVIEW

If you're in a large organization, you may have a file of professionally developed structured interviews that were designed for your jobs and organization. But if you don't have this resource available, you'll need to build your own interviews.

It's tempting to think that you could just keep a list of general questions in your file or cut and paste questions from an Internet site. But if you take interviewing seriously, you (or your organization) must use some form of job analysis or review of job requirements to build a structured interview for each job that you plan to fill.

I like to think of job analysis as the utility tool of human resources. It gives you an understanding of what is to be done on a job. Often, it describes the job setting, tools, and training needed for performing the job. It can also specify the knowledge, skills, abilities, and competencies of a person who can do the job well. All of this is documented in a job description that can summarize the important job information you need for developing your interview questions.

FOCUS ON THE JOB, NOT THE PERFORMERS

It's tempting to think you should study high performers and pick people who are like them. True, this approach will provide some understanding of important job skills and help job experts understand what they are looking for—but it should be used in conjunction with an analysis of the job itself, because it doesn't sample from the broad array of things that need to be done. For example, some high performers do parts of the job poorly, and some poor performers do parts of the job well. The only way to get a complete understanding of required job skills is to focus on the job, not the people doing it.

You may not have access to a job analyst, but you can take a simpler, alternative approach to building a structured interview. It is far from perfect, but it can point you in the right direction.

Here are the basic steps. First, assemble job information, including a job description, a job-analysis report, and lists of job tasks, activities, and

HOW TO BUILD A STRUCTURED INTERVIEW

1. Assemble job information.

   a. Build a file that includes your job description, a job analysis report (if available), and other important information on the job.

   b. Include job information in your file from the O*NET Database, provided by the U.S. Department of Labor.

   c. Ensure that you have listed at least 30 important tasks for the job in your file. Add other job tasks. Rate tasks in terms of importance.

   d. Organize the important job tasks under your organization's competency model or create competencies that reflect job requirements.

   e. Consider talking to job holders and managers, and observe the job being done. Add to or edit your list of job tasks and activities as needed.

2. Meet with job experts and stakeholders.

   a. Document the qualifications of each job expert to show why he or she has expert knowledge of the job. Then have a general conversation about what's important to be done in the job.

   b. Review the information with the job experts and expand the list of tasks if needed. Ensure that the list covers the major dimensions of the job.

   c. Rate the job tasks/activities/competencies in terms of importance and select 10 to 20 of the most important to convert into questions. Exclude questions involving tasks that the person would be trained to do.

   d. Convert the important job tasks and activities into questions and insert them into your new interview during the meeting. Avoid questions about personal traits and personality. Use basic vocabulary.

   e. Ask the job experts to review the interview and "sign off" that it is based on important job tasks/activities/competencies for the job.

3. Write a brief report on the steps you took. Include the qualifications of the job experts, the job information, wish list, notes, and the final interview. Date the report, attach one copy of the interview and keep it in your file.

---

competencies. Second, bring together a group of job experts and get them to review the job information, add to it, and indicate what is important. Third, expand the key words in the job tasks, activities, and competencies into interview questions. There is more guidance in the list of "how to" steps above.

It is important to understand that the structured interview you build should come from the job, not from analyzing the people who are doing the job. Job analysis is systematic and objective, but analyzing people can be influenced by subjective factors such as likability and other personal traits and impressions. The interview should be built solely on objective job requirements.

You can build an interview by converting job tasks, activities, and competencies into questions. For example, here is a job task for a pharmacist:

> Compound and dispense medications as prescribed by doctors and dentists, by *calculating, weighing, measuring, and mixing ingredients,* or oversee these activities.

Interview questions are built from key words in a task, activity, or competency:

> What is your experience *calculating, weighing, measuring, and mixing* pharmacological ingredients?

Notice that the words *calculating, weighing, measuring, and mixing ingredients* are in both the job task and the question.

A similar approach is used when building an interview from job activities and competencies. Look at the example below, and the competency model

---

COMPETENCY ⟶ ACTIVITY STATEMENT ⟶ INTERVIEW QUESTION

The following is a competency, composed of eight activity statements:

1. Follow Procedures: Use work instructions to guide actions; follow policies and procedures even if inconvenient; use work procedures to avoid mistakes; memorize and follow critical procedures and work rules; keep a record that procedures were followed; follow safety procedures in a crisis; distinguish between loose guidelines and strict rules; use policies to guide decision making.

This is one activity statement from the above competency: "Use work instructions to guide actions."

Here is an interview question that was created from the activity statement: "Describe a time when you used work instructions to guide your actions."

Competency models can be built from work activities that represent the broad domain of job activities important for a specific workplace. Interview questions are built from the activity statements that are important for a specific job.

and structured interviews in the Resources section, to get an understanding of how this approach can be used.

The good news is that once you have created the first interview the others will be easier to build. Each interview that you build can be reused until the job changes significantly. Remember that the interview is confidential and should not be posted on the Internet or made available to job candidates. Ideally, you will keep the interviews under lock and key and take them up after they are used.

If you think conducting job analysis and interview building are time consuming and expensive, ask how much it costs to work with someone who should never have been hired.

Finally, I want to point out that you may need to get support from a consultant or expert in human resources. This is particularly true if the job to be filled involves considerations like financial risk, public safety, childcare, or medical services. I am introducing you to a very basic way to create a structured interview, but there are many valuable job-analysis techniques that you would possibly apply with additional help.

SUMMARY

There are many benefits to using a structured, behavior-based interview. It will help you reduce the number of mistakes you make in administering the interview and it will help you feel confident, retain top performers, improve performance, and minimize liability. In the bigger picture, a disciplined approach will help you staff your organization with capable performers.

DURING THE INTERVIEW: DISCOVER WITH DISCIPLINE

With the first interview concluded, the manager turned to me and asked, "How was that?"

"Not bad," I answered. "Let's review.

"You started off well. You put the candidate at ease with a few comfort questions. Then you asked some general information questions about her previous experience and her career goals. You dodged a land mine by not asking about marriage plans or children. That was good.

"You had your questions written down, as we discussed, and you did a good job of staying close to your script. But you slipped in a question that didn't make any sense, and that kind of surprised me. It surprised her, too, and I think that's what you intended to do, to see how she handled it. We call that a 'shock' question. You asked her, 'Which is better, red wine or white wine?' She answered, 'Whichever you like. Some of my friends drink red with everything. I don't care much for alcohol myself.'

"What did you learn from that?" I asked him.

He grinned and said, "I learned that she could handle an unexpected question and stay cool when answering it. I also learned she doesn't drink."

"Is handling a surprise question important in her job description?"

"Well, not really. She won't be in contact with customers. But it tells me she can handle an unexpected situation."

"Maybe," I replied. "But wouldn't it have been more relevant to give her a realistic job situation that might occur unexpectedly, and ask her how she would handle that? Or ask her how she handled an unexpected situation in her previous job?"

"I see your point," he said. "Would've been better just to go straight into the past-event questions, right?"

"You did very well with those, and I noticed that you followed up when you wanted her to clarify her answers. Based on this interview, do you think you could predict how she might perform on the job?"

"Yes, I think so," he answered, "and I'm going to recommend that we hire her."

He thought for a minute, then continued. "I'm beginning to see why you train for the structured, behavior-based interview. My first impression of her was not very favorable. When she came in and we shook hands, there was immediately something about her I didn't like. If I hadn't been so focused on asking past-event questions and writing down her answers verbatim, I might have let that color the whole interview. I might not have discovered just how qualified she was.

"It took me a few minutes," he said, "but I've now figured out what I didn't like about her. Want to know what it was?"

"Tell me."

He said, "She reminded me of the driver who ran into my car last week."

CHAPTER 4

START WITH A GOOD PLAN

An interview rarely ends better than it begins. That's why it's important to plan where you will conduct the interview, how you will meet the candidate, and what you will cover in the first few minutes of the interview.

Even though you have your structured interview ready to use, there is a start-up phase to each interview that is adapted to each specific candidate. It cannot be precisely planned, but you can think over how you will help the candidate feel comfortable, and plan on how you will introduce the interview. You can also plan on what you want to cover regarding the candidate's résumé, career, specialized knowledge, and willingness to do the unpleasant parts of the job.

One of the first things to consider is where to conduct the interview. Will the location be free from interruptions? Is it professional and businesslike? Will the situation be comfortable? Can the interviewer use her structured interview, redirect the candidate when needed, take descriptive notes, and ask reverse questions? Will the situation contribute to the exchange of important information about job skills?

I was once asked to interview a candidate over dinner in a fine restaurant. My client explained that the candidate was a legendary figure in his industry and they didn't want to run the risk of offending him with an interview. I was supposed to use the relaxed setting to develop a "general impression" of how he would fit in the organization. As you can imagine, I passed on the opportunity for a dinner interview because there would have been too many distractions and the results would have been compromised. An effective interview setting has a single purpose, planned questions, and disciplined administration.

Sometimes interviews are conducted in a professional situation but set up with the wrong premise in mind.

- Complimentary interviews may be given to "a friend" when it is clear that he does not have the professional background or experience needed to qualify for the job. As a result, hopes are raised and time is consumed when it would have been better to encourage the friend to consider a more realistic option.

- It is not unusual for an organization to give new interviewers experience by including them on an interview panel. However, sitting in on an interview is no substitute for taking a class with a qualified instructor. In addition, a positive training experience becomes a negative practice when interviews are set up with real candidates for jobs that are not open.

- I know of a candidate who was given a "pretense" interview. He was told that his interview was "just a formality" and that he already had the job. However, his interviewers found him to be somewhat arrogant and not particularly cooperative. When the candidate was hired, the interviewers felt that their findings had been ignored.

- Often a highly qualified candidate is recruited for a job without taking a disciplined, structured interview. The premise is that "we would be lucky to get him," but the conclusion may be "we made a big mistake." Instead of being afraid of losing a strong candidate, insist that he go through the same interviews as other candidates.

If you are conducting a selection interview, the premise needs to be clear. The interviewer is going to meet with a qualified candidate, who is truly interested in the job, and who may get the job. Once you are set on this point, your next task is to manage the first impression of your interview.

MANAGE YOUR OWN INTERVIEW IMPRESSION

Obviously, a lot of energy is directed to how candidates manage their impressions. But it is just as important that you manage the impression created by you and your interview. Consider the idea that a good impression begins with good manners.

- Start on time and end on time.
- Walk to the lobby and greet the candidate by name.
- Escort the candidate to the interview room.
- Treat the handshake as optional—some people don't like it.
- Explain whether the interview will be one-on-one or by a panel.

After the initial meeting, continue to the interview room and ask informal "comfort" questions. They will help you connect with the candidate, set a comfortable tone, and show that you expect to share a productive interview. Then cover the following points in your introduction.

"To start, I want you to know that we are going to have a comfortable and productive time together. I am well prepared for your interview and I have a clear understanding of what the job requires. As you can see, I have a list of questions that will help us explore your skills for the job. Also, I will take notes to help me remember your qualifications.

"I plan to give you my undivided attention. My phone is turned off to minimize interruptions, and I put a note on the door to let people know that an interview is in progress. We will spend about an hour in conversation and wrap up with you having a few minutes to ask me questions.

"So let's get started with the first question. Take about five minutes and guide me through your education and work history."

After your introduction, continue with the interview. Avoid questions or comments with low face validity; proceed with reasonable, job-related questions to discover what the candidate has to offer. For example, you can select from the following types of questions and ask them in a conversational way.

- Willingness questions determine whether the candidate wants to do the job. Often these questions are part of a realistic job preview that highlights the negatives in the job.

QUESTIONS WITH LOW FACE VALIDITY

Projective Questions

"Which is your favorite animal—a skunk or a buzzard?"

"If you were a refrigerator, what would be in you?"

"Answer this: My greatest fear is. . . ."

"Why is rice white?"

"Imagine a room with no light. What is in it?"

"What color best describes your personality?"

"Shock" Problem Questions

"How many honest people are there in the United States?"

"Estimate the number of feathers on a fully grown duck."

"How would you design an elevator that always went up?"

"Why was Zeno's arrow too sharp?"

"List the flavors you taste in cheesecake."

"Why is the positive pole of a battery red?"

"List 10 ways to keep a monkey from scratching."

- Career questions deal with education, past employment, career goals, and special learning experiences.
- Knowledge questions are based on the specific knowledge needed to do a job well. For example, you might ask an accountant questions about generally accepted accounting principles.

Afterwards, you can move into the more formal, structured interview questions.

When you prepare for the interview, remind yourself that it is easy for a well-intentioned, honorable interviewer to misspeak during an interview. So as a precaution, remind yourself to avoid questions that reflect assumptions or stereotypes about groups of people. You'll see a detailed description of "ask" and "don't ask" questions in the Resources section. These are based on the law and reflect the idea that you should ask only questions that directly relate to the job for which the person is being considered.

ASSUMPTIONS, STEREOTYPES, AND QUESTIONABLE QUESTIONS

Assumption or Stereotype	Questionable Question
Older people lack energy.	"Will you need a nap after lunch?"
Persons of color have more conflict with the law.	"Tell me about your arrest record."
Women with children aren't career minded.	"How do you balance family with a full-time job?"
Religious people are easily offended.	"Will you be bothered if we speak of 'the holidays' and avoid 'Christmas' or 'Chanukah'?"

The next section will give you more detail on what questions to ask in the start-up. We will discuss comfort questions, willingness questions, career questions, and knowledge questions.

COMFORT QUESTIONS

Many years ago I got my checkups from a physician who had an office with thin walls. I could hear everything he said in the examining rooms around me. I never once heard a kind word or moment of compassion. It was as though he were running an assembly line, not a service. I decided to look for another physician and soon found one with a sympathetic bedside manner.

Having learned from that experience, I resolved in my own work to create a friendly, supportive environment for job candidates. When a

QUESTIONS TO PUT THE CANDIDATE AT EASE

"Would you like some water?"

"Were your directions to the office helpful?"

"What can I do to make your visit rewarding?"

"What's the weather like in your home town?"

"Did you see the game last night?"

"How long do you plan to stay in town?"

candidate appeared nervous, I tried to be reassuring, but this often wasn't enough. I came to realize that rapport happened mostly when the candidate was talking, not me. This led me to ask comfort questions to get the candidate relaxed and talking about casual topics.

I've seen hundreds of interviewers struggle to connect with a candidate. They know what they want, but not how to get it. I've also seen how quickly they can learn to ask comfort questions. These are trivial and easy to answer—but they help the candidate feel good about talking. And yes, you should avoid comfort questions about legally sensitive topics such as family, child care, lifestyle, and age.

A TWO-WAY CONNECTION

It's up to you to help the candidate feel comfortable, confident, and informed. The foundation for comfort begins with a face-to-face greeting and continues with comfort questions, the introduction to the interview, and the transition into specific questions. If you don't prime the pump at the start, you may find yourself trying to get answers from a dry well.

Comfort questions are only a part of building rapport. Good manners go a long way. I usually walked to the lobby to escort the candidate to the coffee station and into the office. If someone else ushered the candidate in, I always stood when the person entered the room. There's also value in being perceived as a credible interviewer. Your organization, focus, and direction serve to help the candidate feel confidence in your professionalism.

Avoid doing things that create discomfort. Some people don't like to shake hands. Women may feel that this is mainly a male tradition. Different nationalities may feel that any touch is too personal. And yes, a few may be concerned about germs. This can all be resolved by waiting to see if the candidate extends a hand.

I believe that rapport is a want, not a need. I'm not saying that it's okay to be insensitive, but I've conducted many effective interviews with candidates who were nervous wrecks. The candidate can be tense for innumerable reasons that you can't fix. Some people just don't relax, but that's not a major problem. Your task is to get information on job-related skills, not to do interview therapy.

Don't let rapport building dominate the interview. There is a point at which continuing to build rapport just limits the time you have for getting information. After the first few minutes, you should be in rapport maintenance. If you don't have rapport within a few minutes of sitting down, you probably won't get it.

Some interviewers place a great stock in seating arrangements. The standard advice has been to avoid placing a barrier between you, such as a desk or coffee table, and to minimize your authority by being on the same level as the candidate. In both cases, I feel that a lot of unnecessary attention is being wasted on minor issues.

Instead of following rigid rules, just use common sense. If the candidate is tense, take a chair alongside. If the candidate is hostile, put a desk between you. If the candidate is arrogant, maximize your authority. Being responsible for the success of the interview means selecting the approach that best fits the situation. Your primary objective is to get information that predicts job performance, not to arrange the furniture.

WILLINGNESS QUESTIONS

Sometimes a candidate is able, but not willing, to do a job. It could be high-paying but undesirable work—cleaning a sludge pit, working the night shift, perhaps making a two-hour commute. There are all kinds of reasons why a person might not want to do a job that he could do well.

One time I noticed a flight attendant wearing latex gloves during meal service, something I had never seen done before. My curiosity got the best of me; I asked him why. "You know," he said, "people put some pretty nasty

---

WILLINGNESS QUESTIONS

"This job requires you to do an inventory count on New Year's Eve. Are you willing to do this?"

"On this job you will transport people who are very ill. Are you willing to transport patients with contagious diseases?"

"If you start with us, you will have to work the night shift for at least two years. Is this acceptable to you?"

"It is necessary for you to get continuing education on your own time and expense. Are you okay with this?"

"As manager, you will need to clean the restrooms when employees don't show up. Are you willing to clean restrooms?"

stuff on their food tray!" Enough said. He was aware of a real but unpleasant part of his work and accommodated to hold the job.

Here's where the realistic job preview enters the picture. The candidate is shown exactly what she is going to be doing on the job—sometimes in writing, occasionally on video, but often in just an oral explanation. "Realistic" means "no sugar coating"—the good and bad parts of the job are described. Some would call it de-recruiting.

One of the objectives of the realistic job preview is to reveal or describe enough of the distasteful components of the job to show the candidate what she's getting into. If the candidate then chooses to not proceed with the interview, that's fine. A turnover statistic has been avoided, and the position remains open for someone willing to do all parts of the work.

This reminds me of how a friend interviewed household workers. From time to time the housekeeper would have to do distasteful jobs, and my friend felt it best to put this fact on the table. He would explain all the things to be done on the job, including taking the trash to a dump that "just smelled awful." If the candidate resisted, an offer was not made.

Willingness questions educate the candidate quickly on what will actually be done on a job. Then, if a candidate is willing to do all parts of the job, it's time to explore career, education, and goals.

CAREER QUESTIONS

Career questions cover information that is important for putting the candidate's work life into perspective—things such as past jobs, education, and goals. Obviously, this may use up just three or four minutes with a fresh college graduate. A candidate with an extensive work history will take longer.

Career questions can spark your curiosity about the candidate's life. I once heard a man talk about spending a year in a Tibetan monastery after graduating from college. I immediately had a vision of him seated in front of the Dalai Lama, waiting for months to ask a question. But I let this pass. Of course I was curious about his experiences, but probing into religious topics during a secular interview was out of bounds. My job was to get information about his skills as a corporate trainer.

Along this line of thinking, you may wonder how to deal with candidate comments that you don't want to hear. I've heard a lot of things that were important to the candidate but not to the job—losing a child,

CAREER QUESTIONS

"Start with your first job and give me a brief review of your work history."

"Describe your responsibilities in your last job."

"How has your career prepared you for working with us?"

"Explain what your last job says about your learning needs."

"Describe the career accomplishment that means the most to you."

"Tell me about your biggest career disappointment."

"What part of your education gave you the most career preparation?"

---

coming back from the dead, being a police informant, and undergoing a sex change operation, to name a few. My approach was to show respect, put my note pad down, listen respectfully, and quickly transition to a job question. On the legalities, I am told that we are not responsible for what the candidate says, only for what we say.

Remember that you probably have biases about backgrounds. If you went to public school, you may feel that private schools make people elitists. If you were a navy pilot, you might look down on a pilot with commercial training. If you had a job when you were 12, you may discredit the person who started working at 19. My advice is to focus on getting information on the candidate's experience, and not compare the candidate's career to yours. Make judgments only when you rate the candidate's skills for the job.

Candidates' answers to questions about career goals can surprise you. Ideally, you will hear a realistic, challenging career goal. But you may hear goals about things like hobbies, marathons, and cooking classes. Occasionally, you'll hear a fantasy goal—for example, a 40-year-old who wants to play NFL football.

Whatever the goal is, you have an opportunity to get information about commitment. Instead of asking, "What are your goals?" I would ask a behavior-based question. For example: "What is your primary career goal, and what did you do in the last year to move toward it?" The candidate's past actions shed light on the meaningfulness of his goal.

When asking career questions, you may be tempted to write your notes on the candidate's résumé. After all, it lists the candidate's jobs in sequence, along with information on her education and goals. But if other people see the same résumé, with your notes, you may be creating a bias in another interviewer. If it is your private copy, this may not matter, but as a rule of thumb take descriptive notes on your own structured interview form.

KNOWLEDGE QUESTIONS

The knowledge required to do a job ranges from very common knowledge, such as how to access the Internet, to very complex knowledge, such as knowing how to solve a calculus problem.

The O*NET, developed by the U.S. Department of Labor, has general information on the knowledge required to do a broad range of jobs. For example, the requirements shown below for a registered nurse were adapted from the O*NET.

There are many ways to measure or assess knowledge apart from an interview—from degrees, certification, and tests, for example. However, if there is a need to ask knowledge questions in an interview for a specific job, they can be derived from the O*NET list. Alternatively, you could select a

---

KNOWLEDGE QUESTIONS FOR A REGISTERED NURSE

"Describe something you've done that shows your skill with flexible endoscopes or accessories or related products."

"What experience do you have with floor-grade forceps or hemostats?"

"Tell me about a time when it was challenging to apply a peripheral intravenous catheter."

"This job involves use of nasal, oral, and tracheal suctioning equipment. What is your experience in this area?"

"Tell me about a time when you used your knowledge of therapy and counseling to help a patient or family adapt to a difficult medical problem. What was the outcome?"

"Describe a time when you applied your knowledge of public safety and security to help resolve a very difficult situation."

"Describe something you've done that shows the attention you pay to observing standards to protect your own and others' safety. What type of negative situation did you keep from happening?"

HOW TO START AN INTERVIEW

Preparation is essential for a professional start-up. First, review job information, the structured interview you will use, and the candidate's résumé and general correspondence. Think about the comfort questions you will ask and how you will manage the interview for this particular candidate. Finally, verify arrangements on security, parking, arrival time, and other interviews that may have been scheduled for the candidate. Then, continue to plan as follows:

1. **Greet the candidate.** Meet the candidate in the reception area on time and escort her to the interview room.

2. **Ask comfort questions.** Begin with a comfort question such as "How was your trip here?" Continue with more comfort questions and casual conversation to build rapport.

3. **Transition to the introduction.** Name the job to be filled and explain that you will use a structured interview, minimize interruptions, and take notes. Mention that the wrap-up will include a few minutes to talk about the job.

You can continue the start-up with different types of questions, depending on the candidate and the position. For example, consider asking willingness questions to see if the candidate is willing to carry out the less appealing parts of the job. You could next move to career questions to review the candidate's work history, education, and qualifications. Then, think about asking knowledge questions about professional or technical knowledge needed when doing the job. If knowledge requirements are extensive, develop a separate job knowledge interview.

At this point you can move into asking the past-event questions on your structured interview involving skills and competencies.

---

college textbook that relates to a specific job and then develop knowledge questions from the questions at the end of each chapter. The textbook will also provide the answers.

SUMMARY

We've explored the importance of planning how to start up the interview with individual candidates. This process begins when you select a professional interview setting that will minimize interruptions and focus on selection. Avoid conducting complimentary, training, pretense, or recruiting interviews.

During the start-up you have the opportunity to build a positive impression of the interview and ask comfort questions, career questions, knowledge questions, and willingness questions. Then you can transition into asking the past-event questions on your structured interview.

CHAPTER 5

SEEK BEHAVIORAL PREDICTORS

As a behavior-based interviewer, your job is to use a structured interview and prepared questions to gain descriptions of what a candidate has done in order to predict what he will do. Admittedly, the information you get will not be perfectly reliable and the predictions will not be absolutely exact. But the overall task is clear: gain behavioral predictors that reflect on a candidate's job skills as you minimize generalities, abstract traits, and self-promotion.

There is a problem, however. We can be our own worst enemies when it comes to gaining behavioral predictors. This is because our reactions to the candidate can shut down the process of getting information. For example, here are some of the things I have heard said that closed an interviewer's mind on a candidate:

- He lives with his parents, and is therefore labeled as "too timid."
- Her hobby is hang gliding; she is seen as a thrill addict.

- He looks like the last person who was fired, and is labeled a "bad fit."

Instead of letting our preconceptions steer us in the wrong direction, we need to be open to information about job skills during the whole interview, regardless of how we feel about the candidate.

For many people this is a strange idea. We are told by society to listen to our feelings, to hear the inner voice, to go with our "sixth sense." But our instincts about people are subjective, and it is difficult to defend them, especially in court.

THE INTERVIEWER'S MAIN JOB

To predict job performance, ask job-related questions aimed at getting a representative sample of specific times when the candidate used a job skill. Everything else is secondary.

As we discussed in chapter 1, behavioral predictors are measures of a candidate's past actions that will predict future performance. Each behavioral predictor is based on the description of what was done in an actual place, in real time, when performing a particular task. To gain a behavioral predictor, you need to break away from everyday conversational language and move into a goal-driven interaction that follows a specific series of steps.

SIX STEPS TO GAIN A BEHAVIORAL PREDICTOR

When you gain behavioral predictors about work skills, you are applying one of the most well-grounded concepts in behavioral science. Decades of research on employee selection shows that specific information about past work performance is a reasonable predictor of future performance on the job. In addition, several behavioral predictors offer a basic way to measure interview performance. An interview with 12 questions could yield 12 answers that can be combined into an overall rating of the candidate's performance.

Behavioral questions minimize "fluff" answers.

It's nice to talk about the importance of gaining behavioral predictors, but it is critical to explain exactly what to do in order to get them. Over the years I have gravitated to a list of six things to do. Some of the skills are more important than others, and you don't have to use all of them in exact order with each question. However, it is important to understand

HOW TO GAIN A BEHAVIORAL PREDICTOR

1. Present a behavioral question accurately. Review the question silently, look at the candidate, and ask the question as it is written. You may choose to read the question in a natural, comfortable way that maintains rapport and shows exactly what you want to know.

2. Look for a break in eye contact. Notice that the candidate will look away while thinking of an answer. This is a normal behavior. It is a signal that the candidate is thinking and scanning his past.

3. Wait for the answer. Tension may build during the few seconds of silence it may take for the candidate to think of an answer. Don't be tempted to interrupt the silence and make a comment; accept the silence, give the candidate time to think, and wait for the answer to begin.

4. Listen for a behavioral predictor. A behavioral predictor is a real past action that refers to specific names, times, locations, dates, and numbers. However, it is more than just specific information. It also contains meaningful information about skills and can predict job performance.

5. Clarify if needed. If a candidate's answer is unclear or not meaningful, you can restate the question or ask a follow-up probe: "What was the problem?" "Describe the actions you took." "What were the results?"

6. Take descriptive notes. As the candidate is speaking, take legible notes to document what the candidate says. Be thorough enough so you can remember each answer later. Avoid writing down your opinions or interpretations of the candidate's answers.

---

how each of the steps may be used to gain accurate information to predict job performance.

Step 1: Present a Behavioral Question Accurately

Accidental discovery can sometimes yield big outcomes, but it usually takes a long time for chance to work. Instead, use behavioral questions. These tell the candidate that you are looking for an example of something he did at work. No smoke, no mirrors—just ask for what you need to know.

A behavioral question is an open-ended, singular, past-event question about a time when a person used a skill at work. This approach is different from traditional questioning. Instead of asking a general question about reaching goals, you ask for a specific example of what the candidate did to

TO READ, OR NOT TO READ, THE QUESTION

Some argue that reading a behavioral question sends the wrong message and may interfere with getting to know the candidate. Others say that reading questions helps the candidate understand exactly what the interviewer needs to know. My approach is to present each question as it is written, but in a conversational way. This way I can be fair and friendly to all candidates as we explore job qualifications.

---

achieve a work-related goal. The answer you're seeking is a description of a particular thing that was done in past work that relates to the target job.

A behavioral question is more practical than a traditional question, because it helps the candidate know that you want to hear about a specific experience at work. Time is spent more efficiently because you ask for exactly what you want to know.

Some interviewers will ask, "What if the candidate doesn't have any work experience?" But even a new high school graduate has experience that reflects on work habits. In school, one learns to communicate, show up on time, and perform tasks. So if you can't ask about actual work experience, ask about work skills.

Present each behavioral question as it is written. Even a small change in wording can give the candidate license to talk about personal traits and general experiences. For example, it is easy to accidentally ask about "some experiences" instead of "an experience." Even this minor change can license the candidate to speculate and self-promote. If instead you ask each behavioral question in an accurate, conversational way, you're more likely to gain a behavioral predictor and have a thorough understanding of the candidate's job skills.

Step 2: Look for a Break in Eye Contact

Candidates will almost always look to the side when thinking of an answer to a behavioral question. Sometimes the break in eye contact can be a second or less, but more often it will be one to three seconds. It's rare for a candidate to look away for more than ten seconds.

I don't believe that it matters whether the job candidate looks up, down, or sideways in response to an interview question. You're conducting a selection interview, not assessing a person's psychological makeup or doing psychotherapy. You're trying to assess a candidate's job skills in order to predict job performance.

Some people think breaking eye contact is a sign that the candidate lacks confidence or is fabricating an answer. But a quick look to the side is normal and desirable when candidates are attempting to recall a past event that will match the intent of your question. It is not an indication of deception, weak character, or low self-esteem. Everyone looks away, even when trying to think of an honest specific.

You may be wondering, "What am I supposed to do when I see the candidate break eye contact?" Common sense says that you should not stare at the candidate. Instead, look over your structured interview. Silently reread the question you've just asked and keep it at the top of your mind. This will help you judge how well her response answers your question.

Today's interviewers face new issues concerning candidate preparation and rehearsal. Today there are thousands of behavioral questions on the Internet, hundreds of courses on how to prepare for an interview, and more than 30 books on interview preparation, including my own. So you must be alert to answers that are more like personal advertising than a description of past actions. A break in eye contact can help you here. It may show that the candidate is trying to think of a fresh answer rather than remember a rehearsed sales pitch.

Step 3: Wait for the Answer

After you see the break in eye contact, wait for the answer. The candidate may need several seconds to recall a specific example that will answer your question. If you start talking too quickly, you may interfere with the candidate's mental search for an answer. At this point, silence is golden.

While you're waiting for the candidate to answer, you may feel the tension build. You may worry that the candidate feels pressure, or you may be anxious to keep things moving along. Be patient. Both you and the candidate can handle a little tension in order to let the candidate think of an example that will give information on his job skills.

There's a lot of variability in the amount of "wait time" you have to invest to get a specific. My colleagues and I conducted a study of 51 professionals who responded to past-event questions. One person started to answer in 1 second; another took 2 minutes 13 seconds. The average was about 30 seconds. We will talk later about how to probe to help a candidate

OVER-TALK THE CANDIDATE

The candidate who rambles needs your help. Interrupt the stream of words by starting your next question. Continue until the candidate stops talking, listens, and answers the question.

Most people would say it's polite to wait your turn in a conversation. But what if the candidate is so talkative that you can't get information about the skills he brings to the job? It is to the candidate's advantage for you to get the information you need to assess his job skills, and you should interrupt an overtalkative candidate in order to do so.

---

respond, but the point here is that it is important for you to be able to wait long enough to allow the candidate to think of a specific.

Some find it difficult to wait for an answer. I recall leading an exercise in which the interviewer felt great discomfort with silence. While the candidate was thinking, the interviewer squirmed, used hand-to-face gestures, then interrupted the silence. When asked why, she explained that she felt it was rude to put so much pressure on another person. However, a classmate put it in perspective. He said, "It's not rude to let somebody think!"

Armed with this idea, she stumbled into her own way to accept the silence. She occupied herself by looking over her interview questions and competencies. This enabled her to focus not on her internal tension but on her job as an interviewer.

Sometimes the problem is reversed: rather than being silent, the candidate talks too much. In this case your job is to stop the talking, particularly when the candidate is rambling about ideas or experiences that don't provide information about job skills.

This is the time when you can "over-talk" the candidate. Just start your next question while the candidate is still talking. The candidate will stop, listen to your question, and begin with an answer. I've used this approach thousands of times and never had a candidate say I was being rude or disrespectful. People who are too talkative are accustomed to being interrupted.

Step 4: Listen for a Behavioral Predictor

Behavioral predictors don't just magically appear in an interview. Even with well-written questions, you will often have to help the candidate describe a time when she used her job skills. You may have to explain that

PROBE SELF-DESCRIPTIVE GENERALITIES

Listen for self-descriptive generalities in the candidate's answers. For example,
"I am . . .

flexible"	quick"	cooperative"	detailed"
clever"	persistent"	adaptable"	timely"
forthright"	determined"	sensible"	driven"
neat"	smart"	loyal"	a leader"
motivated"	innovative"	resilient"	stable"

When you hear a generality like one of these, use it in a past-event question:
"Give me an example of an action you took that shows your flexibility."

---

you are looking for an example of a real thing she did at work, then present your question again. Sometimes you may need to reassure and encourage her. But gaining a behavioral predictor often requires more than simply presenting a question and waiting for an answer.

There are several stages you may see as the candidate learns to give performance-predicting answers. First, you must be able to recognize when an answer is promotional or a generality. For example, candidates may promote their positive traits: "I am an innovator," "I am an achiever," or "I am caring." But even if trait answers are part of an honest self-concept, they are not evidence for a skill.

General answers are important to recognize as well. For example (italics mine):

> "Well, let's see . . . one place I worked, people would *often* come to my office and ask questions about how to route *some kinds* of documents. Even though it wasn't my job, I would *usually* end up conducting *a kind of* training session for them, and *if* they commented on this to my boss, I would *now and then* get *some sort of* commendation from him."

The answer may be delivered with confidence, but notice that words like "often," "usually," "if," "now and then," and "some sort of" suggest that the candidate is talking in generalities. A generality has limited value because it does not provide specific information on what the person actually did. A behavioral predictor has specific, meaningful information involving a time, location, date, name, or number. It shows what a person did in a particular situation and lets you predict what he will do in a similar situation.

WAS THE CANDIDATE A BYSTANDER OR A PERFORMER?

Although the candidate may be proud of an achievement, it may have been others who did the heavy lifting. For example, you hear the candidate say, "I was the one who pushed the button to launch the first successful space probe." Hearing this answer stated with conviction, you want to believe it. But then comes reality time. Pushing the button was obviously a small action in a large project. How much of the achievement was contributed by smart colleagues with a clear mission, strong leadership, and plenty of capital? In this case, it is reasonable to probe into the significance of the candidate's actions.

There's a big difference between a specific example and a behavioral predictor. A specific example refers to details like names, times, locations, dates, and numbers, but a behavioral predictor refers to details that will predict job performance. Facts are not enough. For example, attending a concert at Carnegie Hall is not sufficient to show that you have musical talent, and being on a restructuring team does not show that you made a difference. The key is to discover a meaningful action that a person actually took, or an idea that was implemented, that lets you predict job performance. Done predicts do! Or as I like to say, "Actions speak. . . ."

LISTEN FOR SPECIFICS IN AN ANSWER

- **Who:** The name, title, or description of a specific person. For example, the candidate asked the supervisor about the rude customer.

- **What:** A description of any tangible aspect of the situation: a number, such as three people; an address; a measure; or an adjective, such as a red hat.

- **When:** This indicator refers to both clock and calendar times. It could mean a particular time frame, such as a certain day at work, a season, or a time at a particular location.

- **Where:** The location where the action was taken: "in my office," "at the substation," or "at the airport."

- **How:** The level of effectiveness achieved, or the steps that were taken. For example: "First I . . . and next I . . . then I finished the. . . ."

As I pointed out in chapter 1, the chances are that over 90 percent of the time you ask a behavioral question, you will get a behavioral predictor. If you're a well-trained, efficient interviewer, you can get a behavioral predictor every 2½ minutes or so—perhaps 10 to 20 in a one-hour interview. However, not all of these will come out fully developed. To clarify, you may need to ask follow-up probes.

Step 5: Clarify If Needed

I've been astonished over the years at how often able candidates gave answers that didn't relate to my questions. Sometimes they misheard or misunderstood the question, or they were so anxious they began answering without taking time to think. Whatever the cause of an irrelevant answer, it's up to you to clarify what was actually done.

There are several scenarios when it makes sense to clarify. For example, if a candidate cannot think of a specific, you could clarify by restating or paraphrasing the question. Or you could clarify when it is not clear that the candidate is giving a specific. In this case, it makes sense to ask questions like "Who was involved?" "What did you do?" or "When did this happen?" These follow-up questions will help you establish that you are hearing a description of a real event.

Probing also makes sense when candidates give nonspecific answers that reflect their self-concept. For example, you ask, "What specific thing did you do on your last job that got you positive recognition?"

The candidate replies, "I was recognized for being flexible in the way that I respond to customers."

Then you probe by asking, "What specific thing did you do with a specific customer that demonstrated flexibility?"

"WHAT" OVER "WHY"

Instead of asking "why" an action was taken, ask "what" was done. A question that begins, "Why did you . . . ?" invites the candidate to speculate and justify the reasons for her actions. "What did you do . . . ?" questions lead to a description of behavior that is useful in evaluating answers. Once you find out what was done in a specific situation, you have descriptive information that will help you measure the candidate's skills. But, when you ask for the reason an action was taken, you're more likely to hear self-promotion or self-justification.

After the answer emerges, you next have the option of asking a reverse probe to gain a broader sample of information about the candidate's work experiences. For example:

"Give me a specific example of a time when you were not flexible with a customer."

Another option is to watch for nonverbal signs of positive and negative feelings as the candidate answers: a facial expression, a hand gesture, or a body shift can signal that there's more to the answer. This is especially important when a nonverbal signal doesn't match the answer. When this happens, just rephrase the written question and ask it again. Don't ask about the feeling, just ask about what the person did in the situation. That will often give you more information.

Step 6: Take Descriptive Notes

Note taking is one of the most difficult skills to master. We know we can't remember everything a candidate says, but you will have to use his answers to rate job skills. There's also the practical fear that you may

---

The SHARE model can help you take relevant, job-related notes. It consists of five topics that you can listen for in an answer and include in your notes.

- **S**ituation is the context of action. Write down what was done, where it was done, when it was done, and who did it. For example, you can ask, "Tell me what you did in this situation."

- **H**indrance shows that there was a difficulty in the situation that required a solution beyond simple problem solving. Here you could ask, "What was a hindrance or challenge you faced?"

- **A**ction indicates that the candidate did something that could lead to a result or outcome. The event was not trivial. Here is a reasonable probe you might ask: "Describe the actions you took."

- **R**esult means that the actions led to an outcome that would show whether the actions were effective. For example, "What were your results?"

- **E**valuation is the candidate's assessment of the results coming from her actions. Was there impact? A probe you could ask here is "How do you evaluate what was achieved?"

This approach lets you take notes on each answer to help you remember most of what was said later, when you are evaluating the candidate's responses.

have to read your notes aloud in court. This is why some attorneys advise interviewers to not write down anything that was said during the interview.

On the other hand, it is reasonable to take notes that relate directly to skills and job tasks. The notes should be descriptive and free of your opinions and interpretations. Write down only what the candidate says that relates to your questions or the job. This will support your own objective thinking and help you remember the answers after the interview when you rate the candidate's job skills.

Here's a more conservative solution to the note-taking dilemma: just write down exactly what the candidate says. Put it in quotes to show this. Don't write down your personal opinions or subjective judgments—only what the candidate says. This is the approach used by psychologists when they administer oral exams. It is also the note-taking technique employed by professional assessors, who are trained to use highly defensible assessment procedures. This technique enables you to assemble objective, descriptive information that is free from your interpretations.

SUMMARY

A behavioral predictor is a specific action that a candidate took which provides evidence that he has a skill that is important for a particular job. It is a measure of a candidate's demonstrated job skills.

Each behavioral predictor is based on the candidate's description of what was done at an actual place and time when performing a particular task. However, to gain a behavioral predictor you will need to break away from everyday, conversational language, and move into a goal-driven interaction that follows six steps:

1. Present a behavioral question accurately.

2. Look for a break in eye contact.

3. Wait for the answer.

4. Listen for a behavioral predictor.

5. Clarify if needed.

6. Take descriptive notes.

By following these steps you should be able to gain 10 to 20 behavioral predictors in a one-hour interview. This will provide the foundation for making your selection decision.

CHAPTER 6

FINISH WITH A NIMBLE WRAP-UP

You may have conducted a spotless, information-laden, high-rapport interview, but if you don't do an effective wrap-up, you can lose your positive momentum and de-recruit an ideal candidate. On the other hand, a good wrap-up advances positive feelings and can generate a lasting favorable impression. You must prepare to make this happen.

There is a clear challenge for you to meet. You have just a few minutes to finish the interview on time while being relaxed, and to answer the candidate's questions without seeming rushed. There is no exact formula on how to make this transition, but it is clear that if you fail, others will hear about it and you may have a negative write-up on one of many Internet sites.

The wrap-up is easier today because most candidates will accept your using a structured interview and taking notes. They will also want to be treated the same way as the other candidates—similar questions, similar interview time, similar standards for evaluation, and so forth. Nevertheless, by the end of the interview they will expect to have individualized treatment, just when you need to move on to other responsibilities.

I see the wrap-up of the interview as being a nimble unwinding, not a thorough debriefing. Yes, you do have to respond to the major questions that the candidate has about the job, but your main job as the interviewer is to get accurate information about the candidate's job skills in order to predict future job performance. This limits the time you can spend answering the candidate's questions.

It would seem that wrapping up an interview would be pretty easy to do. We move from one conversation to another all day long. But there's a difference here: the interview is usually more of a one-way exchange than a two-way conversation. It's logical that you will feel okay with this—you are the interviewer—but most candidates don't feel good about just answering your questions and leaving. They have questions, too, and it's important to think through how you handle them.

To some extent your wrap-up strategy is determined by the situation. If your organization values efficiency, you will be guided by its norm of moving candidates quickly through the screening process. A more relaxed organization will place more value on the perceptions of candidates and encourage you to take your time with each person. As a result, you will need to choose ideas from this chapter that will work for you in your situation.

As you plan your wrap-up, keep in mind that you will need to distinguish between your measurement and relationship objectives. Effective measurement of a candidate's job skills requires you to commit a significant portion of your interview time to getting information. But building a positive interview relationship means giving information to the candidate.

WHAT WOULD A CANDIDATE THINK AFTER YOUR INTERVIEW?

"If we had started on time, I could have asked some questions."

"He did all the talking. There was no time for me."

"At first, things were relaxed, but then we ran out of time."

"There were too many interruptions for him to know about me."

"It looks like I'll be interviewing into the night."

"When I get home, I'm going to burn this place on the Internet."

Effective interviewers recognize both of these objectives and set expectations that put them in balance.

SET EXPECTATIONS UP FRONT

The need to meet an interview's measurement and relationship objectives was once a struggle for me. But things got a lot easier when I realized that if I set expectations in the start-up, then the wrap-up would be easy.

Begin the interview with an indication that you are well prepared. Say that you have a clear understanding of the job, and explain that you will work from a list of job-related questions. Then, at the end of the introduction, be clear about how the wrap-up will flow. For example: "We will spend about an hour in conversation and will wrap up with you having a few minutes to ask me questions."

Notice that the message is clear—there will be "a few minutes" after the interview for you to answer questions. This means some time, not plenty of time. Also, the implication is that this approach is beneficial to the candidate because you are effectively managing the time that you will share in the interview.

Here are a few guidelines to consider when it comes to meeting the candidate's expectations on getting questions answered:

- Talk about what the job involves, working conditions, and policies. Or, explain the interview process and mention upcoming interviews and who will be there. Be clear and to the point without coming across as impatient or rushed.
- Avoid giving feedback on how well the candidate did in the interview. You will need time to evaluate answers and you may change your thinking based on the input of other interviewers. If you feel that you must give feedback, postpone it until after the person is hired.
- Remember that your job is to assess the candidate's skills, not to be a career counselor. Your tips could be very helpful, but the time that you spend coaching is time that you are not gaining behavioral predictors. Save the coaching for later.
- Recognize that your feedback may give the candidate tips on how to answer questions in the next interview. Don't give the candidate new "selling points" for your colleagues' interviews.

By now there is a little voice in your head that is saying, "But what about building a relationship with the candidate? We need to be constantly recruiting." And I agree—partly. It is important to build a relationship with candidates that will support recruiting, but recruiting is a very different aspect of the selection process. Consider the possibility that you may be recruiting a person before you know if she really has the skills needed by the job. Stay focused.

WHY IS TIME SO IMPORTANT IN THE WRAP-UP?

It's easy to lose track of time, especially when you have a very interesting candidate. That's why I put a desk clock between a candidate and myself. At any moment I could see how much time we had left without looking at my wristwatch and alerting the candidate to my time sensitivity. The clock also told me when to speed up the interview.

It can be tempting to give the candidate all the time he needs at the end of an interview. Yes, it is good to be responsive and helpful with the candidate's questions, but there can be unintentional and negative consequences to an extended wrap-up.

- A candidate was given lengthy feedback and felt so positive that he quit his current job before he discovered that he would not get an offer.

- Four interviewers were liberal with their wrap-up time, which made the last interview of the day rushed at 6:30 instead of deliberate at 4:30.

- The candidate got mixed messages when an interviewer gave positive feedback in the morning but the hiring manager later gave average ratings in the afternoon.

Avoid extended wrap-ups and their consequences. Be mindful and professional in your wrap-up.

Lead into the Wrap-up

The way that you introduce the wrap-up is important. As the interview draws to a close, summarize what you have covered and test for thoroughness. Here's one of my favorite ways to do this: "We've gone through a lot of information on your skills for this job. Now let me ask, what should I have asked but didn't?"

This wording would sometimes prompt the candidate to give a spoken summary of the interview. Afterward, he would continue with a comment about not covering a specific point that he wanted to make. Naturally, you would make some time to allow the candidate to answer his own question. Pay close attention, continue to take notes, and continue with your wrap-up.

Every time I used this approach, I sensed that the candidate appreciated my willingness to listen to a question he was asking. It seemed that sharing control of the interview, even for a few minutes, created a good feeling and closure.

Sometimes you will get questions about salary, benefits, and the workplace. My suggestion is to postpone any conversation about salary if you are not the hiring manager or the HR representative. A casual comment here can harm the negotiation process. Your comments about benefits are probably not as impactful, but it is best for them to be explained by someone who has a detailed knowledge of them.

"DID I GET THE JOB?"

During your wrap-up a candidate may ask if he "passed" the interview or can expect a job offer. Here you can point out that the hiring team will make the decision and you have not had time to evaluate the candidate's answers. In some cases, you could also say that there are other candidates for the job and that it is not possible to say who will get it.

It's good to answer questions about the organization's commitment to employee respect and community service. Here you should describe what is done without trying to "sell" a program. For example, although you may have personal opinions about programs involving diversity, college tuition, community relations, aid for the homeless, and other issues, limit yourself to explaining what the program is and how it operates. Let the candidate draw her own conclusions.

Invite Questions

There are ways you can offer to answer the candidate's questions. Consider which of the following phrases works best for you:

"We have a few minutes. What questions do you have about the job?"

"What do you feel you should have told me but we didn't get around to discussing?"

"We've covered a lot, but I suspect we could have missed something. 'What else should we talk about?"

"Now it's your turn. We have a few minutes—what do you want to ask me?"

"Before we move on, do you have a question about your next step?"

This brings us to a sensitive issue. When you invite questions at the end of the interview, some candidates will ask for advice on their own self-development. There may be questions like these:

"Can you tell me what I need to work on?"

"What do you think my top skills are?"

"How can I interview better?"

"What types of training should I get?"

"Will you share your general impressions of me?"

It is best not to give candidates feedback on their personal development. To begin, you can't answer these questions effectively because you haven't rated the candidate's skills, and you can't speak for others on the interview team. What if another interviewer got negative information that you didn't hear about? Then there's time. It takes a minimum of 15 to 30 minutes to deal with these questions. This is time that is subtracted from your time to get behavioral predictors and assess the candidate's job skills.

Another problem is that giving personal growth feedback requires you to provide the person with both positive and negative observations—but there is a dilemma. Your positive feedback may cause the candidate to assume that he will get the job. Then, if he doesn't, he may feel that your positive comments were insincere. Or if you give negative feedback and the candidate does not get the job, he may blame you for a negative recommendation. No matter how you approach personal growth feedback for a candidate, you can lose.

HOW TO STOP THE INTERVIEW

Sometimes a candidate just keeps talking when it is time for you to stop the interview. When this happens, express your appreciation for the candidate's time and walk to the door. This is one interviewing technique that works all the time—no candidate wants to sit in your office alone!

THE TWO-WAY INTERVIEW

An alternate approach to interviewing, called a "two-way interview," lets you answer a candidate's questions as the interview progresses. The interviewer

HOW TO WRAP UP AN INTERVIEW

1. Begin the interview on time. If you don't start on time, the candidate may resent your stopping on time. If there is an interviewing team, ensure that all of the interviewers know their start and stop times.

2. Set the candidate's expectations. Your interview introduction should indicate how much time you will spend in the interview and that there will be "some time" in the wrap-up for you to answer questions.

3. Tell the candidate when the wrap-up begins. Lead into the wrap-up with a phrase that feels comfortable to you, and indicate that you will allow a few minutes to answer questions. Listen attentively.

4. Answer questions directly and briefly. Focus on answering questions about what the job involves, working conditions, and policies. Avoid giving the candidate feedback on interview performance, personal growth tips, or career direction.

5. Explain what will happen next. Describe the next steps in your screening process. This may include future interviews, testing, meeting colleagues, or an employment letter. Respond to questions about the process.

6. Stand up and walk to the door. Thank the candidate for her time and indicate that you have another responsibility on your calendar. Give the candidate your business card.

7. File your interview notes. Ensure that your notes are legible, and make additional notes if necessary. Prepare to rate the candidate's performance and file your notes and ratings afterwards.

---

and the candidate take turns asking each other questions. The interview may take 1½ to 2 hours and offers a pleasant exchange and a lot of sharing. It is valuable when interviewing a highly qualified or talented candidate who should be treated as a potential colleague.

With the two-way approach, the interviewer begins by asking a question about the candidate's job skills. Then the candidate asks a question about things like the work culture, opportunities, and working conditions. The interview continues as the interviewer and the candidate swap questions. The result is a conversational interview, with the interviewer's structured questions built into it. This type of interview is interactive, flexible, and job-related. It enables you to get the information you need while treating a talented candidate like a colleague.

PUT THE WRAP-UP IN PERSPECTIVE

The wrap-up is the last stage of an interview. Here's how it fits into the flow of a one-hour interview.

1. **Greet the Candidate (1–3 minutes)**

   Meet the candidate in the reception area on time and escort him or her to the interview room.

2. **Ask Comfort Questions (3–5 minutes)**

   Ask comfort questions such as "Would you like coffee?" Continue with casual conversation. Avoid legally protected topics.

3. **Transition to the Introduction (1 minute)**

   Name the job to be filled. Explain that you will use a prepared, structured interview, minimize interruptions, and take notes. Then set the expectation that the wrap-up will be a few minutes to talk about the job.

4. **Optional Questions, Depending on the Candidate**

   a. Consider a transition to willingness questions (1–5 minutes). Test for willingness to do the unpleasant parts of the job.

   b. Consider a transition to career questions (5–10 minutes). Explore career experience, education, and qualifications.

   c. Consider a transition to knowledge questions (5–10 minutes). Ask about professional or technical knowledge needed to do the job.

5. **Ask 10 or More Past-Event Questions (35–45 minutes)**

   Gain behavioral predictors in order to measure job skills and predict job performance.

6. **Finish the Interview (5–10 minutes)**

   Ask whether you covered enough information to give a reasonably accurate picture of the candidate's job skills, then allow a few minutes to answer questions about the job.

In about one hour you can do a complete interview, depending on your use of optional questions.

Just to be clear, I think that the two-way interview works best when interviewing executives, senior managers, and professional colleagues. It takes more time than a standard structured interview, but it allows the interviewer to ask all of the structured questions and probe without making the candidate feel that the interview is a one-way ordeal.

SUMMARY

We have explored how to give a brief, time-conscious wrap-up of a selection interview. Allow some time to answer the candidate's questions about the job and interviewing process. Do not give feedback on how well the candidate did in the interview or provide coaching on developmental areas. It makes the wrap-up easier if you set expectations at the beginning of the interview on what will be accomplished.

PART THREE

AFTER THE INTERVIEW:
RATE AND
RESPECT

The sales manager said, "Do we really need to wade through this laborious process you've laid out? I think it's pretty clear who we want to hire."

"Look at it this way," I replied. "All four candidates have left the building. Now you've got to make your decision based solely on what you learned in the interviews. And the only tangible evidence you have left is your notes. Do you think you could go into a court of law and wing it, with nothing to refer to but your memory of things that were said some time ago?"

"No, but we're not going to court."

"Probably not," I said. "But to be completely fair, you need to conduct the rest of this hiring process the same way you conducted the interviews—equally and fairly.

"Without verbatim notes to refer to, your last interview may be the one you remember best. Without notes, your first interview may be the one that lingers in your mind because of something about the applicant that appealed to you. But no matter what the case, your fairest and most

85

balanced judgment comes into play when you follow exactly the same routine with all candidates, treating them equally after they're no longer here to answer questions. You've got to think of what's fair for the candidate, fair for the company, and defensible in a court of law.

"That's why the two-step process I've outlined may seem repetitive and boring to you, but it's the fairest and most efficient way to be sure you make the right decision.

"Read each competency, the rating anchors, and your notes. Then decide how well the information in the notes matches the definition of the competency. It's simple, but it's repetitive. After a little practice, you'll be doing it in a smooth, systematic way.

"This process may simply reinforce your decision that a particular candidate is best for the job, but it may also remind you of some significant factors you may have forgotten or overlooked, and it may even cause you to change your mind."

The sales manager smiled ruefully. "I know you're right, but it's like knowing you've got to eat your spinach before you get your dessert."

"I agree," I said, "but after a while you may actually start to enjoy your spinach.

"There's no guarantee that you'll always make the right decision, but this will greatly increase your chances of hiring the most qualified candidate. And that's the best dessert of all."

7

Rate, Discuss, and Decide

Over a 20-year period I did thousands of selection interviews for all sorts of jobs in every type of work imaginable. Looking back on the experience, I can't remember one assessment that was easy. Regardless of the job or who was being assessed, I grappled with being accurate and fair. But my biggest concerns revolved around rating the candidate's answers and making a recommendation.

It is my goal to help you avoid the struggles I experienced but still benefit from them. When you have mastered this chapter, you will be able to use one competency rating technique that you can learn quickly, apply reliably, and use confidently. It is so practical that it grew to be my favorite approach because it was effective with a wide range of competencies and easy to explain to hiring managers and new interviewers.

As I explain competency rating, you will see that there is a big difference between rating competencies and scoring competencies. When rating, you show your evaluation of the candidate's answers by check marks, symbols, or letters.

A CONCERN WITH SCORING INTERVIEWS

I once saw an interview team use their scoring system to evaluate candidates. One candidate had an interview score of 91, another 76, and so on. Then there was the person at the bottom—a lonely 28. He was dismissed as a "loser" with no recognition that he was strong in managing details. In contrast, the 91 was given lavish compliments with no recognition that he was an impulsive decision maker.

The conclusion: A high interview score can become a positive label and mask a negative quality, and a low interview score can become a negative label and mask a positive quality. As an alternative, the two-step process will allow you to sort out and use all of the information in a candidate's responses before you make a decision.

Then you compare the quality of the answers to job requirements and make a decision. In contrast, a score uses numbers to show your evaluation of answers. Scores can be used in formulas that make the hiring decision, but any time you use numbers you probably should engage consultants who are experienced in this area to help you develop a scoring system.

We will explore how you can use the two-step process, which I have found to be simple and inexpensive to use. It will systematically manage all of the information gathered in the interview and summarize it for you. You will be able to see a profile of the competency ratings for the candidate, then use the ratings to guide your recommendations. This approach can also be used by small organizations with limited resources, or by multinational companies with large budgets.

THE TWO-STEP PROCESS

The two-step process involves (1) reading the competency, rating anchors, and notes, then (2) deciding on the degree to which the information in the notes matches the definition of the competency.

To use the two-step process, you must have a structured interview similar to the salesperson interview that begins on the right and continues on the next three pages. I included an entire interview (without room for notes) to ensure that there was no doubt about what I was talking about. Please follow along as I point out the ways that this interview format supports the two-step process.

CONFIDENTIAL STRUCTURED INTERVIEW*
Salesperson

Candidate: _____ Interviewer: _____ Date: ____ / ____ / ____

Directions: Place a check mark next to each question as you ask it. Ask follow-up questions, if needed, by restating the question or part of it. Take brief notes to summarize each answer. After the interview, check the rating box (below) for each job skill/competency that shows the amount of evidence you got for the skill in the candidate's answers.

Competencies   Rating Anchors

The competencies are not ranked in order of importance. The full competency definition is at the top of each group of questions.	Little Evidence for the Skill	Between	Some Evidence for the Skill	Between	Strong Evidence for the Skill
Influence					
Goal Setting					
Task Orientation					
Productive Coping					
Service Orientation					
Organizational Savvy					

____ **Career/Training Question:** Please give me a quick overview of the work you have had that relates to this job. Also, indicate what certifications, licenses, or degrees you have that reflect on your qualifications to do this job.

---

* This interview is presented as an example only. Before use, the questions and scoring process should be evaluated for use in a particular situation by using generally accepted procedures for developing a selection tool.

Structured Interview, Salesperson (continued)

INFLUENCE: Able to help external customers reach their goals by influencing their decisions. Influence involves such things as qualifying the receptivity of a customer, getting appointments, asking good questions, listening, talking about specific needs, being clear on the features and benefits of a course of action, and maintaining credibility.

_____ 1. Describe a situation when you were effective in getting an appointment with a potential customer. What did you do?

_____ 2. When were you effective in getting a customer to talk about specific needs rather than generalities?

_____ 3. What was a good question that you used with customers to advance a sale?

_____ 4. How did you convert the features of a service into a benefit that was valuable to a customer?

GOAL SETTING: Able to set and work toward challenging, specific, and realistic goals. Outcome goals, with deadlines and measures of success, are best used when the task is simple for the individual or a matter of effort and persistence. Learning goals are the best choice when dealing with complex tasks that require new skills of the individual.

_____ 5. When did you set a challenging, specific, and realistic sales goal? What was the outcome?

_____ 6. Describe an important sales goal and deadlines you worked toward. What results did you achieve?

_____ 7. What was a complex task you had to deal with, and what did you need to learn to achieve it?

_____ 8. When did you learn new skills to reach a challenging goal? What was the goal, and what did you do?

Structured Interview, Salesperson (continued)

TASK ORIENTATION: Able to put extra effort to achieve work tasks and objectives. Achievement motivation is shown by working long hours or weekends and making sacrifices to reach goals. Actions reflect drive and initiative, assuming moderate risk, putting work first, multitasking, and exceeding expectations.

_____ 9. When did you put extra effort into getting your job done? What did you do, and what were the results?

_____10. Describe a time when you made a sacrifice to meet sales or customer deadlines.

_____11. Tell me when you put your work first, even when it was inconvenient for you.

_____12. How did you multitask when dealing with several responsibilities at the same time? What was the result?

PRODUCTIVE COPING: Able to respond to rejection or criticism in a productive, healthy way. It involves putting the stress aside and converting destructive energy to productive energy that is directed to work motivation, positive self-talk, building new work habits, steady performance, and cognitive reframing. Stress is deflected by managing one's reaction to it.

_____13. When were you personally rejected or criticized by a customer? What was the result?

_____14. Tell me how you put customer stress aside and converted destructive energy into productive energy.

_____15. Describe a work experience that shows what you did to be a steady performer in a difficult sales situation.

_____16. What was a new work habit that you developed in order to adapt to stress?

Structured Interview, Salesperson (continued)

SERVICE ORIENTATION: Able to adapt to the changing needs of an external customer by listening to customers, anticipating problems, taking ownership of a problem, tailoring a solution, being timely, meeting expectations, and asking for feedback on service rendered.

____17. When did you anticipate a customer problem and deal with it before it became a serious issue?

____18. When did you tailor-make a solution to fit a customer's needs? What did you do and what was the result?

____19. When did you resolve a customer problem by just listening? Be specific.

____20. When did you get negative feedback on meeting a service promise? How did you apply what you learned?

ORGANIZATIONAL SAVVY: Able to use informal communications and networks to get work done. This includes exchanges with sources of influence, good timing, and listening to people "in the know." Navigating work through an organization requires sensitivity to the agendas of key decision makers, being flexible, and protecting confidential information.

____21. How did you use "organizational savvy" to read the unspoken problems surrounding a sale? What was the situation, and what happened?

____22. When did you work around an organizational roadblock or informal network to make a sale? What did you do?

____23. Describe how your good timing of a sales effort with a specific customer earned you a nice sale?

____24. When did your relationship with a key decision maker allow you to be trusted with confidential information?

THE TWO-STEP PROCESS

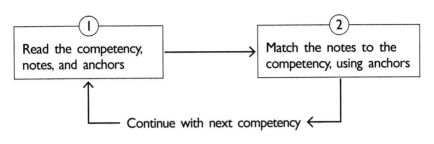

Rating Interview Answers. The first page of the structured interview has a rating template that you can use to show the match of the candidate's answers to each competency. The top of the template has a row of rating anchors to help you evaluate the answers. Notice that the anchors range from "Little Evidence for the Skill" to "Strong Evidence for the Skill."

The wording of the anchors is important. They point you toward rating the evidence that you have for each competency, one at a time. You are not rating the candidate as a person. You are combining the candidate's answers and using the anchors to show the extent to which they provide evidence for the skill.

The names of the competencies to be evaluated in the interview are listed on the left side of the template. They are not ranked in order. They refer to the full definition of each competency on the following pages of the interview. There you will see four questions listed beneath each competency, with a place to check off each question after you ask it. Since these questions are close together, it would be necessary to take your notes on a separate page.

Begin the two-step process immediately after you wrap up the interview. First read (to yourself) the full competency definition, all of your notes, and the rating anchors to ensure that you are focused on them and that they are clearly understood. To practice these steps, please take a few moments now to go back and read the full definition for influence (second page of the interview) and the rating anchors (first page). If there were notes on this interview, you would also read all of them at this time.

I like to emphasize the importance of reading all of the notes before you rate a competency. Any of the candidate's answers could provide information on the candidate's skill in influencing. For example, answers to questions about other competencies like "service orientation" and "organizational

THE COMPETENCY IS YOUR RATING STANDARD

A single answer may provide positive evidence for one competency and negative evidence for another. Consider Task Orientation: Suppose the candidate gave an example of how she made a sacrifice to meet a task deadline—but the same answer also showed that she did not follow important policies and procedures as she worked. So, one answer could provide strong evidence for task orientation and little evidence for policies and procedures. The conclusion is that the competency is the standard for evaluating an answer.

---

savvy" could provide information about the candidate's ability to influence. You have to read all of the notes each time you rate in order to capture the information provided in the entire interview.

Next, you would put a check in the box in the template that shows how strong the evidence (in the notes) is for each competency. Again, note that you would go through the two-step process separately for each of the competencies.

The two-step process does not tell you whether you should recommend or not recommend the candidate. It does provide you with a summary of the information that you have about the candidate and the job. To make your decision, review all of the information you have, including your interview ratings, the candidate's work history, knowledge and skills with job tools, the job analysis, and recommendations. Continue reviewing until you have a recommendation in mind and can explain it in a reasonable way.

If you can't make a recommendation and explain it, review your findings with others on the selection team until you have a basis for your recommendation. Selection decisions are often based on the pooling of all information about a candidate's fit to the job, not a single interviewer's competency ratings. Also, you learn from this approach. You will refine your own judgment on who to hire as you learn how colleagues make their recommendations.

Before we go further, I want to point out that each of the questions in the interview has a direct link to the wording in the competency above it. Look at the competency definition titled "Influence." Find the words "getting appointments." Then look at question number 1 and find the phrase "getting an appointment." You see that the wording of the competency matches the wording in the question. This is not an exact match, but close enough to say the question links to the competency.

THE SELECTION BLENDER

In making selection decisions, think of yourself as a blender. Instead of whipping up a milkshake, you blend information about a candidate until you have convergence on what it all means. Sometimes you will have a nagging thought that won't blend into your recommendation. When this happens, just start the blender again by reviewing the competencies and notes. Continue until you resolve your thinking.

This linkage of questions to competencies is important. The competency represents a skill or ability that is required in order to do the work, and the question is designed to reveal if the candidate can perform that part of the job. This linkage is true for all of the competencies and questions in this interview. It also provides an indication that the interview question can be traced back to job requirements, an important factor in the defensibility of the interview.

MAKE THE TWO-STEP PROCESS WORK FOR YOU

The two-step process is only as effective as your skills as a behavior-based interviewer. Yes, it is important that you use a systematic process to rate competencies, but it is equally important to have reliable, job-related information to use with the process. The two-step process will not do all of the work for you. You will have to feed it with good information and pay close attention as you follow each step.

Here is what you have to put into the process. To begin, you must have a well-crafted structured interview. You won't get very far if you have "soft" competencies that are full of platitudes and general traits of the successful person. It is best to have behavioral competencies that describe what a person does when using the competency. Go to part D of the Resources to see what I mean.

Next, you have to have good questions and be prepared to present them accurately. Over the years I have found that interviewers are tempted to over-adapt questions into their own words. Yes, it is important to make the interview a natural conversation. You can do this by being careful not to read questions in a robotic way. Instead, present the questions naturally without changing their wording.

It is also important to ask reverse questions in order to get a representative sample of information about the candidate's skills. For example, let's

USE A REPRESENTATIVE SAMPLE OF INFORMATION TO RATE SKILLS

If you saw a friend only when he was in a good mood and positive, you might draw the wrong conclusions. The same goes for interviewing. If you allow the candidate to give you only positive information, then your ratings might be one-sided. The solution is to ask reverse questions and gain examples of past actions that are representative of the positive and negative aspects of a candidate's skills.

---

assume that you asked the candidate, "When did your creativity pay off for you?" If the response is similar to other answers, too good to believe, or too promotional, you could ask a reverse question: "Tell me about a time when you tried to be creative but got disappointing results." Then you could get a different example of past behavior that would help you get a representative sample of information about job skills.

It is critical that you have descriptive notes of the important things that the candidate says in response to your questions. When I say descriptive notes, I mean that you write down only what the candidate says. Use quotation marks to show that you are just documenting an answer. Then, after the interview, you can rate the candidate's competencies. You will not be able to remember 10 to 20 examples in a candidate's answers, but you'll be able to recall all the answers when you review your notes.

DISCIPLINE IS CRITICAL

Knowing the two-step process is not enough to make you a good interviewer; discipline in following the procedure is critical. To produce effective ratings, you have to carefully go through the same steps you have been through many times before.

A participant in one of my interviewing classes asked a question that you may be struggling with now: "Doc, let me get this straight on how you rate answers. I read a competency I'm already familiar with, go over notes that I just took, and review anchors that I have used many times before. Then I repeat the very same steps for the other competencies I need to rate. That will take me an extra 7 to 10 minutes after each interview. Is this really necessary?"

My response seemed to surprise him.

"Yes," I said. "But you left something out. You have to really concentrate on what you're doing. It's like paying close attention to each car you see when you drive home the same way every day. If you don't make yourself notice the traffic, you will arrive home but not remember the trip."

I performed this two-step process thousands of times when rating competencies. Yes, it was boring. I had to make myself pay attention, postpone other work, and ignore the phone, but I followed the process. When I evaluated a candidate's answers, I read the same competencies over and over again and concentrated on their exact wording. I marked my notes to

> Resist the temptation to cut the two-step rating process short. Instead, put the procedure to work for you.

link them to the competencies. Sometimes I read the anchors aloud, just to ensure that I was not letting my mind wander. This level of discipline does not require a lot of brainpower, but it does require commitment to a process that you believe in.

Think of the two-step process as a tool that will help you manage the information overload faced by all interviewers. In a one-hour interview, an interviewer can be expected to pose at least 10 past-event questions, ask 20 follow-up probes, and hear at least 10 answers. Along the way she needs to maintain rapport, take notes, ask reverse questions, avoid legally protected topics, answer questions herself, and represent the employer well.

When the interview is over, the interviewer needs to compare the detailed information she gathered to the competencies using a five-point rating scale; then she explains her recommendation to a selection team who will build consensus on hiring the candidate. The two-step rating process will help her manage all of these expectations and information about the candidate in a prudent, effective way.

THE TEAM DECISION

Selection teams make many of today's hiring decisions. A typical team may consist of the hiring manager, the HR manager, the recruiter, a consultant, and a future co-worker; it may include well-trained interviewers, seasoned executives, and investors. It will probably reflect multiple dimensions of diversity and can meet face-to-face, by telephone, or over the Internet.

It is important for your selection team to have an understanding of how it will operate. With so many perspectives in the room, it is important to have a leader who gets consensus on the structured interviews to

HOW TO RATE THE CANDIDATE'S ANSWERS

- Use a well-designed structured interview with questions organized under competencies, a place for notes, and a rating template with anchors to guide your ratings.

- Begin rating immediately after the interview. Don't try to complete the ratings while the interview is in progress. Remind yourself that you must objectively use interview information and minimize subjective impressions and biases.

- Rate the first competency. Read over the competency definition, then review your notes and compare them to the competency using the rating scale anchors. Check the box in the rating template that shows the match of the notes to the competency.

- Continue with the other competencies; repeat the above steps with each. Notice that you must re-read all of your notes each time you rate another competency. Give your full attention as you read the competency, your notes, and rating anchors.

- Resolve rating dilemmas. If you don't feel confident about a rating, continue the process until you have resolved your dilemma. Leave the rating box blank if you cannot develop confidence that your rating is accurate. In the team discussion, learn how others made their ratings.

- Prepare for a selection team discussion. Review the profile of your ratings and look for highs and lows. Think of answers you heard that determined the level of your ratings. Decide whether you will recommend, or not recommend, employment.

---

be used, various schedules, how the team meeting will proceed, and how decisions are made. There must also be a team understanding with regard to confidentiality, ethics, and legal constraints.

I was once part of a team that selected professionals for high-paying jobs in a top corporation. It was my job to conduct assessments of each of the candidates and report the results back to the team. Each of the people in the meeting had either interviewed the candidates or evaluated their technical knowledge and skills. Each meeting took about 2½ hours, during which we reviewed the findings on 10 to 15 candidates. The manager of the group was in charge of the meeting and made the final decision.

This hiring team operated according to the following expectations:

- Each interviewer would use a structured interview and be prepared to comment on interview findings.
- The team leader would choose a candidate to discuss and ask for comments. He took notes on a white board to summarize the competency ratings and comments.
- As the only industrial organizational psychologist in the group, I explained my findings first and presented the results of my interviews and testing.
- The other assessors presented their evaluations of the candidates and sometimes freely disagreed with the manager, other interviewers, and me.
- If there were no disagreement, someone on the team would express some possible concern about the candidate, just to ensure that all candidates were scrutinized.
- The team leader took notes on the comments. After 10 to 15 minutes he summarized the comments and offered his decision.
- The team was invited to rebut the decision. If there was a concern, the conversation continued until the team leader made the final decision.

These team meetings were professionally handled. There were no side discussions about sports, gossip, or corporate politics, and no jokes or disrespectful comments about any of the candidates. Each review was conducted as if the candidate were in the background listening to the conversation. In short, the team was absolutely focused on information about each candidate's skills for the job.

Summary

The two-step process is a systematic way to rate a candidate's skills for a job. In order to use this approach, you must have a structured interview with competencies written in behavioral language, a series of past-event questions organized under each competency, descriptive interview notes, and a rating template with anchors that will help you evaluate the candidate's answers.

This approach to evaluating a candidate's interview performance is relatively simple to understand, but it can be difficult to discipline yourself to follow the steps of the process. You will be tempted to cut the process short, partly because it will take several minutes and partly because it requires you to pay close attention to the information you are using. The reward, however, is being able to explain your ratings in an objective and reasonable manner.

NOTES

1. The following references list some of the published research and books dealing with interview effectiveness.

    Campion, M. A., Campion, J. E., & Hudson, J. P. (1994). Structured interviewing: A note on incremental validity and alternative question types. *Journal of Applied Psychology, 79*, 998–1002.

    Green, P. C. (2007). *Get talent: Interview for actions, select for results.* Memphis, Tenn.: SkilFast.

    Green, P. C., Alter, P., & Carr, A. F. (1993). Development of standard anchors for scoring generic past-behaviour questions in structured interviews. *International Journal of Selection and Assessment, 1*, 203–212.

    Huffcutt, A. I., Roth, P. L., & McDaniel, M. A. (1996). A meta-analytic investigation of cognitive ability in employment interview evaluations: Moderating characteristics and implications for incremental validity. *Journal of Applied Psychology, 81*, 459–473.

    Janz, T. (1982). Initial comparisons of patterned behavior description interviews versus unstructured interviews. *Journal of Applied Psychology, 67*, 577–580.

    Janz, T. (1989). The patterned behavior description interview: The best prophet of the future is the past. In Eder, R. W., & Ferris, G. R. (Eds.), *The employment interview: Theory, research, and practice* (pp. 158–168). Newbury Park, Calif.: Sage Publications.

    Janz, T., Hellervik, L., & Gilmore, D. C. (1986). *Behavior description interviewing: New, accurate, cost effective.* Newton, Mass.: Allyn and Bacon.

    McDaniel, M. A., Whetzel, D. L., Schmidt, F. L., & Maurer, S. D. (1994). The validity of employment interviews: A comprehensive review and meta-analysis. *Journal of Applied Psychology, 79*, 599–616.

    Motowidlo, S. J., Carter, G. W., Dunnette, M. D., Tippins, N., Werner, S., Burnett, J. R., & Vaughn, M. J. (1992). Studies of the structured behavioral interview. *Journal of Applied Psychology, 77*, 571–587.

    Orpen, C. (1985). Patterned behavior description interviews versus unstructured interviews: A comparative validity study. *Journal of Applied Psychology, 70*, 774–776.

    Pulakos, E. D., & Schmitt, N. (1995). Experience-based and situational interview questions: Studies of validity. *Personnel Psychology, 48*, 289–308.

    Schmidt, F. L., & Hunter, J. E. (1998). The validity and utility of selection methods in personnel psychology: Practical and theoretical implications of 85 years of research findings. *Psychological Bulletin, 124*, 262–274.

2. Green, P. C. (1999). *Building robust competencies: Linking human resource systems to organizational strategies,* San Francisco: Jossey-Bass.

3. The following studies provide information regarding the importance of using a structured interview.

Campion, M. A., Palmer, D. K., & Campion, J. E. (1997). A review of structure in the selection interview. *Personnel Psychology,* 50, 1–46. (See p. 34.)

Cronshaw, S. F., & Wiesner, W. (1989). The validity of the employment interview: Models for research and practice. In Eder, R. W., & Ferris, G. R. (Eds.), *The employment interview: Theory, research, and practice* (pp. 269–281). Newbury Park: Sage Publications. (See p. 272.)

Harris, M. M. (1989). Reconsidering the employment interview: A review of recent literature and suggestions for future research. *Personnel Psychology,* 42, 691–726. (See p. 713.)

Huffcutt, A. I., & Arthur, W. (1994). Hunter and Hunter (1984) revisited: Interview validity for entry-level jobs. *Journal of Applied Psychology,* 79, 184–190. (See p. 188.)

Huffcutt, A. I., Conway, J. M., Roth, P. L., & Stone, N. J. (2001). Identification and meta-analytic assessment of psychological constructs measured in employment interviews. *Journal of Applied Psychology,* 86, 897–913. (See p. 897.)

Mayfield, E. C. (1964). The selection interview: A re-evaluation of published research. *Personnel Psychology,* 17, 239–260. (See p. 253.)

McCarthy, J. M., Van Iddekinge, C. H., & Campion, M. A. (2010). Are highly structured job interviews resistant to demographic similarity effects? *Personnel Psychology,* 63(2), Sum 2010, 325–359.

McDaniel, M. A., Whetzel, D. L., Schmidt, F. L., & Maurer, D. D. (1994). The validity of employment interviews: A comprehensive review and meta-analysis. *Journal of Applied Psychology,* 79, 599–616. (See p. 599.)

McMurray, R. N. (1947). Validating the patterned interview. *Personnel,* 23, 263–272. (See p. 272.)

Schmidt, F. L., & Hunter, J. E. (1998). The validity and utility of selection methods in personnel psychology: Practical and theoretical implications of 85 years of research findings. *Psychological Bulletin,* 124, 262–274. (See p. 267.)

Schmitt, N. (1976). Social and situational determinants of interview decisions: Implications for the employment interview. *Personnel Psychology,* 29, 79–101. (See p. 89.)

Ulrich, L., & Trumbo, D. (1965). The selection interview since 1949. *Psychological Bulletin,* 63, 100–116. (See p. 112.)

Wagner, R. (1949). The employment interview: A critical summary review. *Personnel Psychology,* 2, 17–46. (See p. 42.)

Wright, O. (1969). Summary of research on the selection interview since 1964. *Personnel Psychology,* 22, 391–413. (See p. 408.)

4. Hunter, J. E., Schmidt, F. L., & Judiesch, M. K. (1990). Individual differences in output variability as a function of job complexity. *Journal of Applied Psychology,* 75, 28–42.

5. The EEOC information on illegal questions is presented on its website under "Frequently Asked Questions." An integrated summary of this information is provided in Resource A: Lawful and Unlawful Interview Questions. This information was kindly provided to me by a representative at the Equal Employment Opportunity Commission. An Internet search will also give you listings of lawful and unlawful questions as provided by consultants, educators, and attorneys. This information is subject to change.

6. Williamson, L. G., Campion, J. E., Malos, S. B., Roehing, M. V., & Campion, M. A. (1997). Employment interview on trial: Linking interview structure with litigation outcomes. *Journal of Applied Psychology,* 82, 900–912.

RESOURCES

RESOURCES

A. LAWFUL AND UNLAWFUL INTERVIEW QUESTIONS

The EEOC's information on lawful and unlawful pre-employment inquiries is organized under the FAQ (frequently asked questions) section of its website (see www.eeoc.gov).

The information desk was able to provide the following information. It was edited and minimized by the author to deal only with the guidelines of the EEOC that directly related to interview questions. This summary may be incomplete or inaccurate due to changes in policy and the law.

Pre-Employment Inquiries (General)

As a general rule, the information obtained and requested through the pre-employment process should be limited to those essential for determining whether a person is qualified for the job. Information regarding race, sex, national origin, age, and religion are irrelevant in such determinations.

Employers are explicitly prohibited from making pre-employment inquiries about disability.

Although state and federal equal opportunity laws do not clearly forbid employers from making pre-employment inquiries that relate to or disproportionately screen out members based on race, color, sex, national origin, religion, or age, such inquiries may be used as evidence of an employer's intent to discriminate unless the questions asked can be justified by some business purpose.

Therefore, inquiries about organizations, clubs, societies, and lodges of which an applicant may be a member, or any other questions that may indicate the applicant's race, sex, national origin, disability status, age, religion, color, or ancestry if answered, should generally be avoided.

Similarly, employers should not ask for a photograph of an applicant. If needed for identification purposes, a photograph may be obtained after an offer of employment is made and accepted.

Pre-Employment Inquiries (Race)

In general, it is assumed that pre-employment requests for information will form the basis for hiring decisions. Therefore, an employer should not request information that discloses or tends to disclose an applicant's race unless it has a legitimate business need for such information.

If an employer legitimately needs information about its employees' or applicants' race for affirmative action purposes or to track applicant flow, it may obtain the necessary information and simultaneously guard against discriminatory selection by using a mechanism such as tear-off sheets. This allows the employer to separate the race-related information from that used to determine whether a person is qualified for the job.

Asking for race-related information on the telephone could probably never be justified.

Pre-Employment Inquiries (Height and Weight)

Height and weight requirements tend to disproportionately limit the employment opportunities of some protected groups; unless the employer can demonstrate how the need is related to the job, it may be viewed as illegal under federal law. A number of states and localities have laws specifically prohibiting discrimination on the basis of height and weight unless based on actual job requirements. Therefore, unless job-related, inquiries about height and weight should be avoided.

Pre-Employment Inquiries (Credit Rating or Economic Status)

Inquiries into an applicant's current or past assets, liabilities, or credit rating, including bankruptcy or garnishment, refusal or cancellation of bonding, car ownership, rental or ownership of a house, length of residence at an address, charge accounts, furniture ownership, or bank accounts generally should be avoided because they tend to impact minorities and females more adversely. Exceptions exist if the employer can show that such information is essential to the job in question.

Pre-Employment Inquiries (Religious Affiliation or Beliefs)

Questions about an applicant's religious affiliation or beliefs (unless the religion is a bona fide occupational qualification [BFOQ]), are generally viewed as non-job-related and problematic under federal law.

Religious corporations, associations, educational institutions, and societies are exempt from the federal laws that EEOC enforces when it comes to the employment of individuals based on their religion. In other words, an employer whose purpose and character is primarily religious is permitted to lean toward hiring persons of the same religion. This exception relieves religious organizations only from the ban on employment discrimination based on religion. It does not exempt such organizations from employing individuals due to their race, gender, national origin, disability, color, or age.

Other employers should avoid questions about an applicant's religious affiliation, such as place of worship, days of worship, and religious holidays, and should not ask for references from religious leaders, such as a minister, a rabbi, a priest, an imam, or a pastor.

Pre-Employment Inquiries (Citizenship)

Employers should not ask whether a job applicant is a United States citizen before making an offer of employment. The Immigration Reform and Control Act of 1986 (IRCA) makes it illegal for employers to discriminate with respect to hiring, firing, or recruitment or referral for a fee based on an individual's citizenship or immigration status. For example, the law prohibits employers from hiring only U.S. citizens or lawful permanent residents unless required to do so by law, regulation, or government contract; it also prohibits employers from preferentially hiring temporary visa holders or undocumented workers over qualified U.S. citizens or other protected individuals, such as refugees or individuals granted asylum.

Because of potential claims of illegal discrimination, employment eligibility verification should be conducted after an offer to hire has been made. Applicants may be informed of these requirements in the pre-employment setting by adding the following statement on the employment application:

"In compliance with federal law, all persons hired will be required to verify identity and eligibility to work in the United States and to complete the required employment eligibility verification document form upon hire."

Pre-Employment Inquiries (Marital Status, Number of Children)

Questions about marital status and number and ages of children are frequently used to discriminate against women and may violate Title VII if used to deny or limit employment opportunities.

It is clearly discriminatory to ask such questions only of women and not men (or vice versa). Even if asked of both men and women, such questions may be seen as evidence of intent to discriminate against, for example, women with children.

Generally, employers should not use non-job-related questions involving marital status, number or ages of children or dependents, or names of spouses or children of the applicant.

Such inquiries may be asked after an employment offer has been made and accepted if needed for insurance or other legitimate business purposes.

The following pre-employment inquiries may be regarded as evidence of intent to discriminate when asked in the pre-employment context:

- Whether applicant is pregnant
- Marital status of applicant, or whether applicant plans to marry
- Number and ages of children, or future childbearing plans
- Child care arrangements
- Employment status of spouse
- Name of spouse

Pre-Employment Inquiries (Gender)

Questions about an applicant's sex (unless it is a bona fide occupational qualification [BFOQ] and is essential to a particular position or occupation), marital status, pregnancy, medical history of pregnancy, future childbearing plans, number or ages of children or dependents, provisions for child care, abortions, birth control, ability to reproduce, and name or address of spouse or children are generally viewed as non-job-related and problematic under Title VII.

Any pre-employment inquiry in connection with prospective employment expressing or implying limitations or special treatment because of sex (unless based upon BFOQ), or any inquiry made of members of one sex and not the other, is similarly troublesome.

Pre-Employment Inquiries (Arrest and Conviction)

There is no federal law that clearly prohibits an employer from asking about arrest and conviction records. However, using such records as an absolute measure to prevent an individual from being hired could limit the employment opportunities of some protected groups and thus cannot be used in this way.

Since an arrest alone does not necessarily mean that an applicant has committed a crime, the employer should not assume that the applicant committed the offense. Instead, the employer should allow the applicant an opportunity to explain the circumstances of the arrest(s) and should make a reasonable effort to determine whether the explanation is reliable.

Even if the employer believes that the applicant did engage in the conduct for which he or she was arrested, that information should bar him or her from employment only to the extent that it is evident that the applicant cannot be trusted to perform the duties of the position when considering

- the nature of the job,
- the nature and seriousness of the offense, and
- the length of time since it occurred.

This is also true for a conviction.

Pre-Employment Inquiries (Security or Background Checks for Certain Religious or Ethnic Groups)

If the employer requires all other applicants to undergo background checks before being offered a position, the employer may require members of religious or ethnic groups to undergo the same pre-employment investigations.

Of course, as with its other employment practices, the employer may not subject only particular religious or ethnic groups, such as Muslims or Arabs, to heightened security checks.

Some employers, such as defense contractors, may require a security clearance for certain jobs pursuant to a federal statute or executive order.

Clearance determinations must generally be processed and made without regard to race, religion, or national origin.

However, security clearance determinations for positions subject to national security requirements under a federal statute or an executive order are not generally subject to review under the equal employment opportunity statutes.

Pre-Employment Inquiries (Disability)

Under the law, employers generally cannot ask disability-related questions or require medical examinations until after an applicant has been given a conditional job offer. This is because, in the past, this information was frequently used to exclude applicants with disabilities before their ability to perform a job was evaluated.

Employers are permitted to ask limited questions about reasonable accommodation if they reasonably believe that the applicant may need accommodation because of an obvious or voluntarily disclosed disability, or where the applicant has disclosed a need for accommodation.

Employers may ask whether the applicant will need an accommodation to perform a specific job duty, and if the answer is yes, the employer may then ask what the accommodation would be.

The employer may not ask any questions about the nature or severity of the disability.

Medical Questions, Examinations, and Discrimination

The ADA (Americans with Disabilities Act) places restrictions on employers when it comes to asking job applicants to answer medical questions, take a medical exam, or identify a disability.

An employer may not ask a job applicant, for example, whether he or she has a disability or about the nature of an obvious disability. An employer also may not ask a job applicant to answer medical questions or take a medical exam before making a job offer.

An employer may ask a job applicant whether he or she can perform the job and how he or she would perform the job. The law allows an employer to condition a job offer on the applicant answering certain medical questions or successfully passing a medical exam, but only if all new employees in the same job have to answer the questions or take the exam.

Once a person is hired and has started work, an employer generally can ask medical questions or require a medical exam only if the employer needs medical documentation to support an employee's request for an accommodation or if the employer has reason to believe an employee would not be able to perform a job successfully or safely because of a medical condition.

The law also requires the employer to keep all medical records and information confidential and in separate medical files.

B. A STRUCTURED COMPETENCY INTERVIEW FOR A WORKFORCE RECRUITER[1]

Candidate_____   Interviewer_____

Position___Workforce Recruiter_____   Date _____ / ___ / _____

After the interview, use the rating template to assess the candidate's competencies.

Rating Template*

Rating Anchors / Competencies**	Little Evidence for the Skill	Between	Some Evidence for the Skill	Between	Strong Evidence for the Skill
6. Productive Coping					
11. Self-Management					
15. Serve Others					
17. Oral Communication					
18. Respect Diversity					
22. Organizational Savvy					

*   To rate a competency, compare all of your notes with the full competency definition. Then look over the anchors. Continue reviewing the information until you feel you can reliably check the box that best shows the match of the candidate's answers to the rating anchors.

** The competencies are not weighted or ordered by rank. The numbers refer to the number of the competency in the competency model.

Comments_____

_____

_____

_____

_____

☐ Don't hire   ☐ Advance in the process   ☐ Hire

_____

[1] This interview is presented as an example only. Before use, the questions and scoring process should be evaluated for use in a particular situation by using generally accepted procedures for developing a selection tool.

Structured Competency Interview, Workforce Recruiter (continued)

6. Productive Coping: Rebound from conflict, criticism, or rejection; be calm when others are upset or angry; perform reliably under pressure or stressful circumstances; avoid profanity, outbursts, and sarcasm when under pressure; recover quickly after mistakes; show a respectful and positive attitude even under pressure; acquire new habits to adapt to stress; use positive self-talk to cope.

1. Dealing with employers and job candidates can be stressful. Tell me about a time when you were able to rebound from conflict, criticism, or rejection. What did you do to cope productively?

2. In recruiting it's important to perform reliably when under pressure or dealing with stressful circumstances. Describe a work experience that shows what you did to be a steady performer in a difficult situation.

3. Tell me about a time when you held a positive attitude under pressure.

4. Describe a new work habit you learned in order to adapt to stress.

Notes:

Structured Competency Interview, Workforce Recruiter (continued)

11. Self-Management: Work effectively without being supervised; take the initiative and self-manage; direct one's own actions with little guidance; start on time even when working alone; review one's own work independently; correct errors on one's own; manage one's work situation without direction; self-coach or self-direct several times a day.

1. Being an effective recruiter requires self-management. Give me an example of a time when you worked effectively without supervision. What were the circumstances, what did you do, and what were the outcomes?

2. Pick a day in your work and describe what you did to take the initiative and self-manage.

3. Describe a time when you wished that you had more work guidance. What did you do?

4. Self-coaching is an important part of improving your performance when working alone. Tell me how you coached yourself on a specific task at work.

Notes:

Structured Competency Interview, Workforce Recruiter (continued)

15. Serve Others: Anticipate service needs of associates or customers; listen to both facts and feelings on service problems; take ownership of a service problem; meet or exceed service expectations; initiate helpful customer or associate service; follow through on service promises; deliver service results to challenging people; ask for feedback to assess quality of service.

1. As a recruiter, you will deal with customers that include employers, co-workers, and job candidates. In your current work, when did you anticipate one of your customers' needs for service?

2. Listening to a customer is an important part of service. When did you resolve a situation by listening to the facts and feelings around a service problem? What was your approach and what happened?

3. Describe a time when you took ownership of a service problem experienced by one of your customers. What was the problem, what did you do, and what was the outcome?

4. It is challenging to deliver superior service to a difficult customer. When did you do this effectively?

Notes:

Structured Competency Interview, Workforce Recruiter (continued)

17. Oral Communication: Get attention before speaking; speak clearly with understandable meaning; present or speak to groups; ask questions to guide conversation; restate or paraphrase to test for understanding; use grammar and verbal expressions appropriate for the situation; take notes to ensure accurate communications; exchange spoken information accurately.

1. Give me an example of how you skillfully communicated an idea during a presentation or speech.

2. Describe a time when you asked questions in order to guide a conversation. What was the situation, what questions did you ask, and what was the outcome?

3. It is not always easy to be effective in communicating your ideas. Describe a time when you restated or paraphrased to test for understanding. What happened?

4. Sometimes taking notes will ensure accurate communication. When did you get good results from taking notes?

Notes:

Structured Competency Interview, Workforce Recruiter (continued)

18. Respect Differences: Avoid prejudging people; resist using stereotypes in decision making; reject jokes or slurs about diverse groups; treat each person according to his or her individual qualities; give respect regardless of background; use the same standards with all people; correct others on the use of stereotypes; support fair and objective treatment for all.

1. Stereotypes can interfere with making good decisions about people. Tell me about a time when you avoided using a stereotype and looked for reliable information about a person.

2. Describe a situation when you ignored a person's background and gave respect when others didn't.

3. What approach did you use in a specific situation to apply the same standards to evaluate people? What was one of the standards, and how did you use it?

4. It can be risky to correct another person who is using a stereotype. Tell me about a time when you did speak up. How did you minimize the risk?

Notes:

Structured Competency Interview, Workforce Recruiter (continued)

22. Organizational Savvy: Use organizational smarts to get results; use organizational contacts or network to facilitate projects; work around organizational roadblocks, agendas, or politics; test rumors with trusted associates; time efforts based on organizational readiness; identify credible sources of organizational information; share organizational information with trusted contacts; protect organizational secrets and confidences.

1. Recruiting often requires you to be smart in the way that you advance a placement. Tell me about a time when you used organizational smarts to get things done.

2. Describe how you used your contacts to facilitate a work project.

3. When did you work around an organizational roadblock? What did you do?

4. Sometimes it's critical that you protect organizational secrets or confidences. Pick a situation involving a confidence or secret that you can ethically tell me about. What did you do?

Notes:

C. A STRUCTURED INTERVIEW FOR AN ASSEMBLER[1]

Candidate_____   Job applied for__Assembler__

Interviewer_____   Date_____

Instructions: Present each question in order and make notes in the margin using only the candidate's words. After the interview, compare the candidate's answers to the competencies. Show your recommendation in the "don't hire" or "hire" box.

Follow Procedures: Use work instructions to guide actions; follow safety procedures in a crisis.

1. What work instructions did you follow on your last job?
2. Tell me about a time when you followed safety procedures but others didn't.

Focus Attention: Notice warnings or safety indicators; avoid daydreaming during routine work.

3. How did you stay alert to warnings or safety indicators?
4. How did you keep from daydreaming during routine work?

Self-Management: Direct one's own actions with little guidance; start on time even when working alone; correct errors on one's own.

5. What did you do when a supervisor wasn't around?
6. What did you do to start working on time?
7. Tell me about a time when you caught your own mistake.

Planning and Organizing: Project and organize work materials; sort tools for easy access; organize one's workspace to work efficiently.

8. How did you organize your work materials?
9. What did you do to keep your tools handy?
10. Tell me how you organized your work space.

Based on the answers given to the above questions, rate the applicant's competencies by checking the appropriate boxes in this template.

Competencies	Negative Evidence	In Between	Some Evidence	In Between	Positive Evidence	Not Measured
Follow Procedures						
Focus Attention						
Self-Management						
Planning and Organizing						

Recommendation: _____   ☐ Don't hire   ☐ Hire

[1] This interview is presented as an example only. Before use, the questions and scoring process should be evaluated for use in a particular situation by using generally accepted procedures for developing a selection tool.

D. A BEHAVIOR-BASED COMPETENCY MODEL

1. Focus Attention: Pay attention and monitor the work situation; notice warnings or safety indicators; avoid daydreaming during routine work; be alert to changes in the work situation; stay focused and ignore distractions from work; resume attention quickly after a distraction; attend to what is being said and to instructions; be alert to changes in equipment or conditions.

2. Practical Problem Solving: Gather facts or objective information on a problem; recognize feelings that define a workable solution; avoid jumping to a quick or easy solution; build solutions on the causes of problems; get others' input in problem solving; consider the practical constraints on a solution before implementation; launch a practical solution or decision; look for indications of the quality of a solution.

3. Fast, Firm Decision Making: Act quickly, even with incomplete information; make speedy, effective decisions; be decisive in an emergency; make a safety or security decision without hesitation; make a prompt decision when under pressure; avoid rethinking decisions; assume authority to make a time-sensitive decision; make minor decisions automatically.

4. Analytical Problem Solving: Use disciplined research techniques in problem solving; apply math or statistics in technical analysis of a problem; use a database or computer analysis to research a problem; use the scientific method in problem solving; use statistics in problem analysis; plot statistical trends to project problems; collect data on the causes of a problem; project problems caused by solutions; report on problem analysis or recommendations.

5. Deal with Uncertainty: Be cool during uncertainty or change; stay collected and composed in unclear situations; tolerate a lack of direction or planning; resist jumping into action to get closure; work with constant change or unpredictable circumstances; work with shifting priorities without distress; look for opportunities in chaos; be effective in the absence of facts or direction.

6. Productive Coping: Rebound from conflict, criticism, or rejection; be calm when others are upset or angry; perform reliably under pressure or stressful circumstances; avoid profanity, outbursts, and sarcasm when under pressure; recover quickly after mistakes; show a respectful and positive attitude even under pressure; acquire new habits to adapt to stress; use positive self-talk to cope.

7. Goal Setting: Set specific, challenging goals; put goals in writing; stretch skills with challenging goals; get participation in goal setting; write outcome goals for tasks with known steps; set learning goals for complex tasks with emerging steps; set goals with milestones or deadlines; use goals to guide efforts and actions.

8. Individual Planning and Organizing: Use a systematic approach in planning; set priorities to guide scheduling; use a calendar or schedule for planning; forecast work needs for personal planning; do backup or contingency plans; develop or organize work materials for a plan; sort files or tools for easy access; organize one's workspace to work efficiently.

9. Innovation: Offer new or better ways to do things; develop novel products; invent, design, or visualize new concepts or products; create unique written or graphic materials; involve a creative team or experts; be open to new or creative ideas; test or experiment with new concepts or prototypes; get suggestions when creative ideas are tried out.

10. Task Orientation: Take personal responsibility for achieving tasks; complete tasks under difficult or stressful conditions; work hard and persevere on tasks; make sacrifices to meet task deadlines; take a calculated risk in choosing tasks; compete against oneself to improve task performance; show high urgency or task drive; handle multiple tasks or demands.

11. Self-Management: Work effectively without being supervised; take the initiative and self-manage; direct one's own actions with little guidance; start on time even when working alone; review one's own work independently; correct errors on one's own; manage one's work situation without direction; self-coach or self-direct several times a day.

12. Follow Procedures: Use work instructions to guide actions; follow policies and procedures even if inconvenient; use work procedures to avoid mistakes; memorize and follow critical procedures or work rules; keep a record that procedures were followed; follow safety procedures in an emergency; distinguish between loose guidelines and strict rules; use policies to guide decision making.

13. Honesty and Credibility: Stand by convictions and values; follow through on promises; tell the whole truth; be honest and complete in documentation; admit mistakes and accept fault; be a trusted, credible source of information; exemplify core values; use internal values to guide actions.

14. Commitment to Learn: Take classes to develop work skills; continue learning after graduation; learn at conventions and meetings; use a mistake as a learning opportunity; take new work to learn new skills; set aside time every day to learn; acquire new work skills or knowledge continually; read and study educational publications.

15. Serve Others: Anticipate service needs of associates or customers; listen to both facts and feelings on service problems; take ownership of a service problem; meet or exceed service expectations; initiate helpful customer or associate service; follow through on service promises; deliver service results to challenging people; ask for feedback to assess quality of service.

16. Assertion: State an opinion directly and maturely without apology; express feelings without abuse or intimidation; repeat an idea tactfully until it is accepted; say no without guilt; use a reasonable style when disagreeing; avoid being pushy or overly dominant; show confidence and self-esteem through gestures and tone of voice; be direct but tactful on sensitive topics.

17. Oral Communication: Get attention before speaking; speak clearly with understandable meaning; present or speak to groups; ask questions to guide conversation; restate or paraphrase to test for understanding; use grammar and verbal expressions appropriate for the situation; take notes to ensure accurate communications; exchange spoken information accurately.

18. Respect Differences: Avoid prejudging people; resist using stereotypes in decision making; reject jokes or slurs about diverse groups; treat each person according to his or her individual qualities; give respect regardless of background; use the same standards with all people; correct others on the use of stereotypes; support fair and objective treatment for all.

19. Lead and Influence: Read the situation and choose how to lead; use participation to get commitment; use authority to get compliance; lead by creating a shared vision; bargain or negotiate to influence on issues; lead by modeling desired behavior; lead by emphasizing a key idea; use charm and style to influence others.

20. Motivate: Build work motivation in others; recognize performance to reinforce energy and motivation; be an example of work motivation; overlap work and personal goals to motivate; motivate others by showing confidence in their abilities; compliment positive attitude or effort to motivate; use role models as motivational examples; motivate with incentives for good work.

21. Teamwork: Contribute in team meetings and discussions; adopt team goals, roles, and standards; support team morale and continuous improvement; confront performance problems of the team; put informing ahead of criticizing team members; teach skills to team members; avoid negative comments about any team member; support team decisions once made.

22. Organizational Savvy: Use organizational smarts to get results; use organizational contacts or network to facilitate projects; work around organizational roadblocks, agendas, and politics; test rumors with trusted associates; time efforts based on organizational readiness; identify credible sources of organizational information; share organizational information with trusted contacts; protect organizational secrets and confidences.

For special orders and bulk purchases of the *Actions Speak!* book, contact Media Learning International LLC at

www.medialearninginternational.com

To preview the *Actions Speak!* DVD or to place an order, contact Media Partners Inc. toll free at

800.408.5657

or go to

www.media-partners.com

Paul Green invites your questions or comments. Go to contacts at

paulcgreen.com